P9-DWY-085

A LITERARY READER

Latin American WRITERS

nextext

Table of Contents

PART TWO: THE HUMAN LANDSCAPE

PART FOUR: AUTHENTICITY AND REDEMPTION

*Throughout the reader, vocabulary words appear in boldface
type and are footnoted. Specialized or technical words and phrases
appear in lightface type and are footnoted.*

Love and the Battle
of the Sexes

Misguided Men

BY SOR JUANA INÉS DE LA CRUZ

Translated by Margaret Sayers Peden

Sor Juana Inés de la Cruz (Mexico, 1648–1695) was a passionate and controversial nun in colonial Mexico. She is considered the most important literary figure of the Baroque period of Latin American literature. Her intelligence and poetic talent reached far beyond national boundaries, and her work is a cornerstone in the defense of the rights of women to study, teach, and write. De la Cruz is the author of numerous poems and plays as well as the famous "Response to Sor Filotea de la Cruz," in which she denounces a bishop's injunction against her intellectual pursuits. "Misguided Men" is her most popular work. In it she accuses men of forcing women to give up their freedom and censures women for allowing them to do so.

Misguided men, who will chastise
a woman when no blame is due,
oblivious[1] that it is you

---

[1] **oblivious**—unconscious; unaware.

who prompted what you criticize;
    if your passions are so strong
that you elicit their disdain,
how can you wish that they refrain
when you incite them to their wrong?
You strive to topple their defense,
and then, with utmost gravity,
you credit sensuality
for what was won with **diligence**.[2]

    Your daring must be qualified,
your sense is no less senseless than
the child who calls the boogeyman,
then weeps when he is terrified.

    Your mad **presumption**[3] knows no bounds,
though for a wife you want Lucrece,[4]
in lovers you prefer Thaïs,[5]
thus seeking blessings to compound.

    If knowingly one clouds a mirror
—was ever humor[6] so absurd
or good counsel so obscured?—
can he lament that it's not clearer?

    From either favor or disdain
the self same purpose you achieve,
if they love, they are deceived,
if they love not, hear you complain.

    There is no woman suits your taste,
though **circumspection**[7] be her virtue:
ungrateful, she who does not love you,
yet she who does, you judge unchaste.

---

[2] **diligence**—hard work.

[3] **presumption**—arrogance.

[4] Lucrece—noble Roman wife who committed suicide after being raped.

[5] Thaïs—famed courtesan who traveled with the armies of Alexander the Great.

[6] humor—mood.

[7] **circumspection**—discretion; restraint.

You men are such a foolish breed,
appraising with a faulty rule,
the first you charge with being cruel,
the second, easy, you decree.

So how can she be temperate,
the one who would her love expend?
if not willing, she offends,
but willing, she infuriates.
Amid the anger and torment
your whimsy causes you to bear,
one may be found who does not care:
how quickly then is grievance vent.

So lovingly you inflict pain
that **inhibitions**[8] fly away;
how, after leading them astray,
can you wish them without stain?

Who does the greater guilt incur
when a passion is misleading?
She who errs and heeds his pleading,
or he who pleads with her to err?

Whose is the greater guilt therein
when either's conduct may dismay:
she who sins and takes the pay,
or he who pays her for the sin?

Why, for sins you're guilty of,
do you, amazed, your blame debate?
Either love what you create
or else create what you can love.

Were not it better to forbear,[9]
and thus, with finer motivation,
obtain the unforced admiration
of her you plotted to ensnare?

---

[8] **inhibitions**—inner restraints to impulses.

[9] forbear—refrain.

But no, I deem you still will revel
in your arms and arrogance,
and in promise and persistence
adjoin flesh and world and devil.

QUESTIONS TO CONSIDER

1. Why do you think the poet does not clearly name the offense that men commit toward women? What effect does she achieve in this way?

2. The poet appeals to reason in addressing male readers throughout the poem. What evidence in the text suggests that the poet expected her appeal to be successful?

3. This poem was written in the last half of the 17th century. In what ways is the poem relevant today?

Two Words

BY ISABEL ALLENDE

Translated by Margaret Sayers Peden

One of the most famous Latin American women writers, Isabel Allende (Chile, 1942–) is also known for her family connection to former Chilean president Salvador Allende. She and her family were forced to flee Chile when Augusto Pinochet assumed control in 1973. Allende easily established herself in Venezuela, writing for women's magazines and feminist newspapers. She went on to publish such famed novels as The House of Spirits, Eva Luna, *and* Paula. *While she is celebrated for her novels, Allende has also written a number of fine short stories. In "Two Words," Allende depicts a woman's struggle to survive in a world dominated by men and corruption.*

She went by the name of Belisa Crepusculario,[1] not because she had been baptized with that name or given it by her mother, but because she herself had searched until she found the poetry of "beauty" and "twilight"

---

[1] Belisa Crepusculario—the name is loosely based on Spanish words for "beautiful" and "dusky."

and cloaked herself in it. She made her living selling words. She journeyed through the country from the high cold mountains to the burning coasts, stopping at fairs and in markets where she set up four poles covered by a canvas awning under which she took refuge from the sun and rain to minister to her customers. She did not have to peddle her merchandise because from having wandered far and near, everyone knew who she was. Some people waited for her from one year to the next, and when she appeared in the village with her bundle beneath her arm, they would form a line in front of her stall. Her prices were fair. For five centavos she delivered verses from memory; for seven she improved the quality of dreams; for nine she wrote love letters; for twelve she invented insults for **irreconcilable**[2] enemies. She also sold stories, not fantasies but long, true stories she recited at one telling, never skipping a word. This is how she carried news from one town to another. People paid her to add a line or two: our son was born; so-and-so died; our children got married; the crops burned in the field. Wherever she went a small crowd gathered around to listen as she began to speak, and that was how they learned about each other's doings, about distant relatives, about what was going on in the civil war. To anyone who paid her fifty centavos in trade, she gave the gift of a secret word to drive away melancholy. It was not the same word for everyone, naturally, because that would have been collective deceit. Each person received his or her own word, with the assurance that no one else would use it that way in this universe or the Beyond.

Belisa Crepusculario had been born into a family so poor they did not even have names to give their children. She came into the world and grew up in an

---

[2] **irreconcilable**—unable to be brought into harmony or mutual understanding.

inhospitable[3] land where some years the rains became avalanches of water that bore everything away before them and others when not a drop fell from the sky and the sun swelled to fill the horizon and the world became a desert. Until she was twelve, Belisa had no occupation or virtue other than having withstood hunger and the exhaustion of centuries. During one **interminable**[4] drought, it fell to her to bury four younger brothers and sisters; when she realized that her turn was next, she decided to set out across the plains in the direction of the sea, in hopes that she might trick death along the way. The land was **eroded**,[5] split with deep cracks, strewn with rocks, fossils of trees and thorny bushes, and skeletons of animals bleached by the sun. From time to time she ran into families who, like her, were heading south, following the mirage of water. Some had begun the march carrying their belongings on their back or in small carts, but they could barely move their own bones, and after a while they had to abandon their possessions. They dragged themselves along painfully, their skin turned to lizard hide and their eyes burned by the **reverberating**[6] glare. Belisa greeted them with a wave as she passed, but she did not stop, because she had no strength to waste in acts of compassion. Many people fell by the wayside, but she was so stubborn that she survived to cross through that hell and at long last reach the first trickles of water, fine, almost invisible threads that fed spindly vegetation and farther down widened into small streams and marshes.

Belisa Crepusculario saved her life and in the process accidentally discovered writing. In a village near the coast, the wind blew a page of newspaper at her feet. She picked up the brittle yellow paper and

---

[3] **inhospitable**—unwelcoming; unfriendly.

[4] **interminable**—seemingly unending.

[5] **eroded**—worn by wind and weather.

[6] **reverberating**—repeatedly reflected.

stood a long while looking at it, unable to determine its purpose, until curiosity overcame her shyness. She walked over to a man who was washing his horse in the muddy pool where she had quenched her thirst.

"What is this?" she asked.

"The sports page of the newspaper," the man replied, concealing his surprise at her ignorance.

The answer astounded the girl, but she did not want to seem rude, so she merely inquired about the significance of the fly tracks scattered across the page.

"Those are words, child. Here it says that Fulgencio Barba knocked out El Negro Tiznao in the third round."

That was the day Belisa Crepusculario found out that words make their way in the world without a master, and that anyone with a little cleverness can **appropriate**[7] them and do business with them. She made a quick assessment of her situation and concluded that aside from becoming a prostitute or working as a servant in the kitchens of the rich there were few occupations she was qualified for. It seemed to her that selling words would be an honorable alternative. From that moment on, she worked at that profession, and was never tempted by any other. At the beginning, she offered her merchandise unaware that words could be written outside of newspapers. When she learned otherwise, she calculated the infinite possibilities of her trade and with her savings paid a priest twenty pesos to teach her to read and write; with her three remaining coins she bought a dictionary. She poured over it from A to Z and then threw it into the sea, because it was not her intention to defraud her customers with packaged words.

* * *

One August morning several years later, Belisa Crepusculario was sitting in her tent in the middle of a

---

[7] **appropriate**—take into one's possession.

plaza, surrounded by the uproar of market day, selling legal arguments to an old man who had been trying for sixteen years to get his pension.[8] Suddenly she heard yelling and thudding hoofbeats. She looked up from her writing and saw, first, a cloud of dust, and then a band of horsemen come galloping into the plaza. They were the Colonel's men, sent under orders of El Mulato, a giant known throughout the land for the speed of his knife and his loyalty to his chief. Both the Colonel and El Mulato had spent their lives fighting in the civil war, and their names were **ineradicably**[9] linked to devastation and **calamity**.[10] The rebels swept into town like a stampeding herd, wrapped in noise, bathed in sweat, and leaving a hurricane of fear in their trail. Chickens took wing, dogs ran for their lives, women and children scurried out of sight, until the only living soul left in the market was Belisa Crepusculario. She had never seen El Mulato and was surprised to see him walking toward her.

"I'm looking for you," he shouted, pointing his coiled whip at her; even before the words were out, two men rushed her—knocking over her canopy and shattering her inkwell—bound her hand and foot, and threw her like a sea bag[11] across the rump of El Mulato's mount. Then they thundered off toward the hills.

Hours later, just as Belisa Crepusculario was near death, her heart ground to sand by the pounding of the horse, they stopped, and four strong hands set her down. She tried to stand on her feet and hold her head high, but her strength failed her and she slumped to the ground, sinking into a confused dream. She awakened several hours later to the murmur of night in the camp,

---

[8] pension—retirement benefit.

[9] **ineradicably**—permanently.

[10] **calamity**—disaster; tragedy.

[11] sea bag—sailor's duffle bag.

but before she had time to sort out the sounds, she opened her eyes and found herself staring into the impatient glare of El Mulato, kneeling beside her.

"Well, woman, at last you've come to," he said. To speed her to her senses, he tipped his canteen and offered her a sip of liquor laced with gunpowder.

She demanded to know the reason for such rough treatment, and El Mulato explained that the Colonel needed her services. He allowed her to splash water on her face, and then led her to the far end of the camp where the most feared man in all the land was lazing in a hammock strung between two trees. She could not see his face, because he lay in the **deceptive**[12] shadow of the leaves and the **indelible**[13] shadow of all his years as a bandit, but she imagined from the way his gigantic aide addressed him with such humility that he must have a very menacing expression. She was surprised by the Colonel's voice, as soft and well-modulated as a professor's.

"Are you the woman who sells words?" he asked.

"At your service," she stammered, peering into the dark and trying to see him better.

The Colonel stood up, and turned straight toward her. She saw dark skin and the eyes of a ferocious puma, and she knew immediately that she was standing before the loneliest man in the world.

"I want to be President," he announced.

The Colonel was weary of riding across that godforsaken land, waging useless wars and suffering defeats that no **subterfuge**[14] could transform into victories. For years he had been sleeping in the open air, bitten by mosquitoes, eating iguanas and snake soup, but those minor inconveniences were not why he wanted to change his destiny. What truly troubled him was the terror he

---

[12] **deceptive**—hidden.

[13] **indelible**—permanently marked.

[14] **subterfuge**—deception; trick.

saw in people's eyes. He longed to ride into a town beneath a triumphal arch with bright flags and flowers everywhere; he wanted to be cheered, and be given newly laid eggs and freshly baked bread. Men fled at the sight of him, children trembled, and women miscarried from fright; he had had enough, and so he had decided to become President. El Mulato had suggested that they ride to the capital, gallop up to the Palace, and take over the government, the way they had taken so many other things without anyone's permission. The Colonel, however, did not want to be just another tyrant; there had been enough of those before him and, besides, if he did that, he would never win people's hearts. It was his **aspiration**[15] to win the popular vote in the December elections.

"To do that, I have to talk like a candidate. Can you sell me the words for a speech?" the Colonel asked Belisa Crepuscularia.

She had accepted many assignments, but none like this. She did not dare refuse, fearing that El Mulato would shoot her between the eyes, or worse still, that the Colonel would burst into tears. There was more to it than that, however; she felt the urge to help him because she felt a throbbing warmth beneath her skin, a powerful desire to touch that man, to fondle him, to clasp him in her arms.

All night and a good part of the following day, Belisa Crepuscularia searched her **repertory**[16] for words adequate for a presidential speech, closely watched by El Mulato, who could not take his eyes from her firm wanderer's legs and virginal breasts. She discarded harsh, cold words, words that were too flowery, words worn from abuse, words that offered **improbable**[17] promises, untruthful and confusing words, until all she

---

[15] **aspiration**—ambition; hope.

[16] **repertory**—collection.

[17] **improbable**—unlikely.

had left were words sure to touch the minds of men and women's intuition. Calling upon the knowledge she had purchased from the priest for twenty pesos, she wrote the speech on a sheet of paper and then signaled El Mulato to untie the rope that bound her ankles to a tree. He led her once more to the Colonel, and again she felt the throbbing anxiety that had seized her when she first saw him. She handed him the paper and waited while he looked at it, holding it gingerly between thumbs and fingertips.

"What the shit does this say," he asked finally.

"Don't you know how to read?"

"War's what I know," he replied.

She read the speech aloud. She read it three times, so her client could engrave it on his memory. When she finished, she saw the emotion in the faces of the soldiers who had gathered round to listen, and saw that the Colonel's eyes glittered with enthusiasm, convinced that with those words the presidential chair would be his.

"If after they've heard it three times, the boys are still standing there with their mouths hanging open, it must mean the thing's damn good, Colonel," was El Mulato's approval.

"All right, woman. How much do I owe you?" the leader asked.

"One peso, Colonel."

"That's not much," he said, opening the pouch he wore at his belt, heavy with proceeds from the last **foray.**[18]

"The peso entitles you to a bonus. I'm going to give you two secret words," said Belisa Crepusculario.

"What for?"

She explained that for every fifty centavos a client paid, she gave him the gift of a word for his exclusive use. The Colonel shrugged. He had no interest at all in her offer, but he did not want to be impolite to someone

---

[18] **foray**—military raid.

who had served him so well. She walked slowly to the leather stool where he was sitting, and bent down to give him her gift. The man smelled the scent of a mountain cat issuing from the woman, a fiery heat radiating from her hips, he heard the terrible whisper of her hair, and a breath of sweetmint murmured into his ear the two secret words that were his alone.

"They are yours, Colonel," she said as she stepped back. "You may use them as much as you please."

El Mulato accompanied Belisa to the roadside, his eyes as entreating as a stray dog's, but when he reached out to touch her, he was stopped by an avalanche of words he had never heard before, believing them to be an **irrevocable**[19] curse, the flame of his desire was **extinguished**.[20]

* * *

During the months of September, October, and November the Colonel delivered his speech so many times that had it not been crafted from glowing and durable words it would have turned to ash as he spoke. He traveled up and down and across the country, riding into cities with a triumphal air, stopping in even the most forgotten villages where only the dump heap betrayed a human presence, to convince his fellow citizens to vote for him. While he spoke from a platform erected in the middle of the plaza, El Mulato and his men handed out sweets and painted his name on all the walls in gold frost. No one paid the least attention to those advertising ploys; they were dazzled by the clarity of the Colonel's proposals and the poetic **lucidity**[21] of his arguments, infected by his powerful wish to right the wrongs of history, happy for the first time in their

---

[19] **irrevocable**—permanent; irreversible.

[20] **extinguished**—put out.

[21] **lucidity**—clarity.

lives. When the Candidate had finished his speech, his soldiers would fire their pistols into the air and set off firecrackers, and when finally they rode off, they left behind a wake of hope that lingered for days on the air, like the splendid memory of a comet's tail. Soon the Colonel was the favorite. No one had ever witnessed such a **phenomenon:**[22] a man who surfaced from the civil war, covered with scars and speaking like a professor, a man whose fame spread to every corner of the land and captured the nation's heart. The press focused their attention on him. Newspapermen came from far away to interview him and repeat his phrases, and the number of his followers and enemies continued to grow.

"We're doing great, Colonel," said El Mulato, after twelve successful weeks of campaigning.

But the Candidate did not hear. He was repeating his secret words, as he did more and more obsessively. He said them when he was mellow with nostalgia; he murmured them in his sleep; he carried them with him on horseback; he thought them before delivering his famous speech; and he caught himself savoring them in his leisure time. And every time he thought of those two words, he thought of Belisa Crepusculario, and his senses were inflamed with the memory of her **feral**[23] scent, her fiery heat, the whisper of her hair, and her sweetmint breath in his ear, until he began to go around like a sleepwalker, and his men realized that he might die before he ever sat in the presidential chair.

"What's got hold of you, Colonel," El Mulato asked so often that finally one day his chief broke down and told him the source of his befuddlement: those two words that were buried like two daggers in his gut.

"Tell me what they are and maybe they'll lose their magic," his faithful aide suggested.

---

[22] **phenomenon**—rare and extraordinary thing or event.
[23] **feral**—animal-like; savage.

"I can't tell them, they're for me alone," the Colonel replied. Saddened by watching his chief decline like a man with a death sentence on his head, El Mulato slung his rifle over his shoulder and set out to find Belisa Crepusculario. He followed her trail through all that vast country, until he found her in a village in the far south, sitting under her tent reciting her **rosary**[24] of news. He planted himself, spraddle-legged, before her, weapon in hand.

"You! You're coming with me," he ordered.

She had been waiting. She picked up her inkwell, folded the canvas of her small stall, arranged her shawl around her shoulders, and without a word took her place behind El Mulato's saddle. They did not exchange so much as a word in all the trip; El Mulato's desire for her had turned into rage, and only his fear of her tongue prevented his cutting her to shreds with his whip. Nor was he inclined to tell her that the Colonel was in a fog, and that a spell whispered into his ear had done what years of battle had not been able to do. Three days later they arrived at the encampment, and immediately, in view of all the troops, El Mulato led his prisoner before the Candidate.

"I brought this witch here so you can give her back her words, Colonel," El Mulato said, pointing the barrel of his rifle at the woman's head. "And then she can give you back your manhood."

The Colonel and Belisa Crepusculario stared at each other, measuring one another from a distance. The men knew then that their leader would never undo the witchcraft of those accursed words, because the whole world could see the voracious-puma eyes soften as the woman walked to him and took his hand in hers.

---

[24] **rosary**—prayers. In Roman Catholicism, the rosary is a series of prayers honoring the Virgin Mary.

QUESTIONS TO CONSIDER

1. What picture of Belisa Crepusculario's world do you get from the story?

2. Why do you think Allende says that Belisa has withstood "the exhaustion of centuries"?

3. What do you think are the two words Belisa gives the Colonel at their parting? What is their effect?

4. Why would a man such as the Colonel appeal to Belisa? What does she hope for from him?

The Warmth of Things

BY NÉLIDA PIÑÓN

Translated by Helen Lane

A prolific writer since 1981, Nélida Piñón (Brazil, 1936–) has published eight novels and several collections of stories. She is the fourth woman to be named to the Brazilian Academy of Writers. The daughter of Spanish immigrants, Piñón often depicts Brazil's foreign communities in her writing. Her literature also frequently reflects the plight of the poor. "The Warmth of Things" is one of her most well-known works. In this story, a boy undergoes an extraordinary physical transformation, causing him to turn on, and, in some ways, turn into his own mother.

    The neighbors called him "meat turnover." And his mother tenderly repeated: "My beloved meat turnover." The nickname came from the obesity that Oscar never successfully fought off, despite **rigorous**[1] diets. One

---

[1] **rigorous**—difficult; demanding.

time he lived on water for five days, without his body showing any effect of the sacrifice. After that he accepted his exploding appetite and forgot his real name.

From early on, he fell into the habit of calculating his age according to the number of centimeters his rapidly expanding waistline measured, taking no account of how many birthdays he had celebrated with cakes, black bean stew with sausage, and platters of macaroni. So he soon felt old among young people. Especially since he had no clothes that would disguise his bulges. If he would only wear skirts with gussets, he would at least be able to hide those regions of his body that gave him a pie shape.

He constantly rebelled against a fate that forced upon him a body that was such a violent contrast to his delicate, **svelte**[2] soul. Especially when his friends offhandedly admitted that they missed having him along with an ice-cold draft beer. And their only reason for not downing Oscar right there at the table in the bar was their fear of the consequences. But they did nibble at his belly, and tried their best to pry a black olive out of his navel.

The house was gloomy on his birthdays. His mother turned out half the lights. Only the candles on the cake illuminated the presents on the sideboard. Always the same ones: long-handled bath brushes, since his pot belly kept him from reaching his feet, and immeasurable lengths of cloth from the dry goods store. After blowing the candles out, he forced the mirror to show him his face with its innumerable fine wrinkles around his eyes, its drooping cheeks, its multiple chins. He saw that his **extremities**[3] looked as though they had been mashed with a kitchen fork, so as to keep odd bits of ground

---

[2] **svelte**—slender.

[3] **extremities**—limbs; hands and feet.

meat from escaping from the dough consisting of flour, lard, milk, and salt that his body was made of.

Despite his visibly upset feelings with regard to meat turnovers, he ate dozens of them every day. And not being able to find them on every street corner, he tucked in his knapsack a supply of soy oil, a frying pan, turnovers to fry, and a discreet flame to be fed by blowing hard on it. In vacant lots, before frying them, he chased off any strangers who might be out to rob him of his rations.

Each morning when he awoke, his body was different. Perhaps because certain fat deposits shifted to another center of greater interest, around his liver, for instance, or because he sometimes put on four kilos[4] in less than sixteen hours. A physical madness that played its part in stripping him of all pride. Of his pride in being handsome. Unleashing in its stead a great resentment in his heart against the friends who hadn't yet devoured him during that week, despite his closer and closer resemblance to a meat turnover sold on a street corner.

In his hour of greatest sadness he clung to the little medal of Our Lady of Fatima[5] around his neck, under whose protection his mother had placed him, for lack of a patron saint who watched over fat people in particular. At home, he whistled to hide his sorrow. But the tears from some of his fits of weeping flowed so thick and fast that they wet the floor, which his mother happened to be wiping dry at just that moment. She pretended not to notice. Only when his tears formed a puddle, as though rain had leaked through the roof, did his mother go, coins in hand, to special friends of his to get them to accompany Oscar to the movies at least once a month. The ones who agreed to go with him one day were

---

[4] four kilos—about nine pounds.

[5] Our Lady of Fatima—refers to the Virgin Mary, who reportedly appeared in Fatima, Portugal, in 1917.

reluctant to do so the next, despite the lure of the money. And just as she was running out of friends of his to ask, Oscar himself, who no longer fit in any seat, stopped going to movies that he had to watch standing up.

On Sundays, the dinner table was full of smoking platters. Oscar saw himself in the place occupied by the roast, carved with a silver knife and fork, with the whole family in high spirits. In order to avoid such **punitive**[6] visions, he retired to his room on those days.

In summer, his torment grew worse, for instead of sweat, it was oil, vinegar, and mustard, his mother's favorite seasonings, that dripped from his chest. Touched by divine gifts of such a nature, she would then stroke her son's head, pulling out at the same time a few curly hairs, which, once back in her room, she examined one by one, anxious to find out how much longer she would have her son with her at home, safe and sound.

Oscar collected this maternal **consolation**[7] in the same tin he used to store the leftover fat from his **itinerant**[8] frying pan. And, wishing to reward the sacrifice his mother had made by drinking the oil and vinegar from his breast, he beamed a smile at her, whereupon she exclaimed: "What a beautiful smile you have. It's the smile of well-being, my son." These words were followed by ones that wounded him to the quick and which his mother, in tears, could not help uttering: "Ah, my beloved meat turnover!"

The expression of this affection, which his misshapen body could not have inspired, made Oscar creep off to his room, hurt by these **corrosive**[9] words from his mother, whose one aim was to get him inside the red-hot frying pan of her fervor, patience, and hunger.

---

[6] **punitive**—punishing.

[7] **consolation**—comfort; solace.

[8] **itinerant**—traveling from place to place.

[9] **corrosive**—destructive.

He foresaw a tragic end for himself. His friends ready and waiting, like vultures, to peck at his flesh. The prospect of his own pain led him to read on the walls a minutely detailed balance sheet of his credits. He had his doubts about his earthly estate. The column listing his debts had grown so long that he would never free himself of them as long as he lived. He owed his flesh to his fellows, because they were hungry. And even though they owed him a body that he could be proud of, he had no way of getting it from them.

Once he was freshly bathed and smelled of scented lotion, he imagined what love between humans would be like, their bodies lying in the bed unaffected by a lack of control over a hostile obesity. At such moments, misled by the hope of a modest credit balance, he reached the point of being able to see himself doing battle with his **adversaries**.[10] It took no more than a **brusque**[11] gesture, however, for reality to remind him of a **corpulence**[12] in which there was no place for poetry and love. And immediately, the prospect of being eaten with a knife and fork was transformed into the most obscure question.

His mother put up a fight against his wildly staring eyes, his soul continually in mourning. What evil is abroad in the world that makes you look upon us with such suspicion? Oscar gave her a platinum brooch as a present, to be plunged forever into her breast. Drops of poison and the certainty of her own cross to bear were to drip from her flesh. In the face of the **enigma**[13] that Oscar was posing, his mother, who throughout her life had rejected **limpid**[14] phrases, uttered the words, "Oh, such a good meat turnover of a son!"

---

[10] **adversaries**—enemies.

[11] **brusque**—abrupt; abbreviated.

[12] **corpulence**—obesity.

[13] **enigma**—puzzling matter; something inexplicable.

[14] **limpid**—clear and simple.

The more she **extolled**[15] virtues that, in all truth, both of them despised, the more eagerly Oscar hastened to remove from the edges of his body residues that perchance had not fit inside the turnover that he was. In the end he abandoned the vacant lots where he had fried his turnovers. He no longer tolerated being stared at with a hunger that he was unable to satisfy. He had no way to feed the poor. They would have to die without help.

As his consultations of the mirror, a clouded one, grew more intense, the glass gave him only a dim view of his body tailored every day by an efficient kitchen fork. He dressed himself in a turnover every morning. In retaliation, he installed his armchair in the kitchen, leaving it only to sleep. He attended to the basic necessities, and practiced his new habit of sprinkling wheat flour all over his body. With the hollows under his fingernails smeared with fat, he received visitors there, obliging them to smooth his flour-dusted skin.

His mother rebelled against this **uncouth**[16] behavior. She did not want her friends to be exposed to such an ordeal. If he was a prisoner of his obesity, let him put up with it in a dignified manner. Her son returned the insult with his teeth moving like a power saw, nearly grinding her arms to a fine powder. And his performance was so convincing that his mother took to protecting her limbs with thick pieces of wool, despite the heat. She left her face showing. And when Oscar insisted that she stay within reach of his hands, she slunk away underneath the coats and boots.

By the age of thirty, Oscar was fed up. It was his turn now to eat anyone who suggested a turnover. He had been willing to play this role for so long a time that he demanded human flesh to **sate**[17] his appetite. He

---

[15] **extolled**—praised.

[16] **uncouth**—uncivilized; coarse.

[17] **sate**—satisfy.

would select his victim very carefully. Although he was particularly inclined toward people who belonged to the household, **fraternal**[18] blood. And following through with his plans, he pretended to be blind, stumbling over things, so as to distract his enemies. His mother asked the neighbors for help, and they took turns staying with her during the first week, only to leave her by herself after that. With so many things to do, his mother took to wearing light clothing, forgetting her son's threats.

Oscar for his part was surprised to discover the charms of speech. He had never before been heard to hold forth so **rapturously**[19] on objects that in point of fact he claimed he could not see. He had just discovered that he possessed the power to make his hunger **coincide**[20] with a verbal **voracity**[21] that had always been in his blood, but to which he had attributed no importance, occupied as he was in defending himself against those who wanted to fling him into the frying pan.

His mother soon accustomed herself to his blindness. She treated him like a passenger in an endless tunnel. She described the house to him, as though he were a guest in it. She wanted him to participate in everyday life, and her face suddenly brightened on seeing her son's gentleness. That was when Oscar opened his eyes, certain that he had won. And there she was, smiling, her arms outside, her body exposed. He rapidly went over in his memory the times that, moved by the force of love, she had called him her meat turnover, coming close to eating him. At that moment his mother, having suffered for his sake, caught in his eyes a gleam that was not that of a chandelier, or of happiness, or of the remote

---

[18] **fraternal**—of or relating to a brother.

[19] **rapturously**—delightedly.

[20] **coincide**—occur at the same time as.

[21] **voracity**—extreme hunger.

truth of a son she hardly knew. What the mother discovered in her son was a flame bent upon living, and the unmistakable look of an executioner.

She stood there calmly at his side. Oscar would take the necessary steps. She was aware of him as a man for the first time. He drew his armchair closer to his mother's, which she had dragged to the kitchen. He asked her to sit down. He too sat down, after first plucking out a few of the woman's hairs. And only with his mother's consent did he begin to keep a close watch on her.

QUESTIONS TO CONSIDER

1. While some of this story is clearly surreal, what portions of the story seem naturalistic? How do these affect your appreciation of the story?

2. What does Piñón suggest about the world of the story when she refers to Oscar's ability to sweat oil, vinegar, and mustard in hot weather as a "divine gift"?

3. In your opinion, do Oscar and his mother become more, or less, alike at the end of the story?

4. If this story could be thought of as a parable, what do you think Piñón wants to teach or show the reader?

A Little Romance

BY CALVERT CASEY

Translated by John H. R. Polt

Calvert Casey (Cuba, 1924–1969) was born in Baltimore and moved to Havana after the Cuban Revolution in 1959. His body of work is limited to two short collections of stories and a volume of criticism. Despite having written only a few works, Casey has earned an international audience and gained acclaim for the introspective nature of his compositions. In "A Little Romance," Casey's disoriented protagonist struggles to make sense of the world he can't possibly understand.

Monday

Last night I spent a long time sitting in Philosophers' Park. Nobody knows that that park where Luz Caballero sits meditating as he faces the Avenida del Puerto, his elbow resting on his knee, with a bust of Saco on one side and one of Padre Varela on the other, is Philosophers' Park. Just as nobody knows that the name of the park with the amphitheater is, or ought to be, Greek Park, because it has paths where you can meditate and statues. One fell over, or they took it away, because it's gone. Just the empty pedestal is left, but I like it that way. Nobody knows that, because when you get right down to it nobody knows anything. Just as nobody knows, either, that behind the park there used to be a promenade[1] called Cortina de Valdés, or that a hundred years ago the house with the Gothic arches used to be a monastery.[2] But of course nobody knows it, because as I said, nobody knows anything.

I was out of breath when I got to the park. I'd been walking all over the old part of Havana. All the benches were taken by young couples. I rested for a bit on some free space on one of the benches and then went over to the carnival they've set up across the street. Something unexpected and very enjoyable happened to me there. By chance I got into a conversation with two girls. They were neither pretty nor ugly, but they were nice. They were having a heated argument about the shortest way to Casablanca. I explained it to them, but so as not to lose their company I convinced them there was nothing there. That left them not knowing what to do; and since I had nothing more to say to them, or, it seemed, they to me, I invited them for a ride on the Ferris wheel. I hardly ever do such things; but I suddenly thought that's the way really good times begin, with an invitation to ride on the Ferris wheel. Afterwards they let me treat them to an ice cone, because that's all you can get there. Then we went for a ride in those little electric cars that bump into each other to scare you and make you laugh, although nobody's scared. The three of us wouldn't fit, so they started to argue about who'd go with whom till I stepped in once more, took the chubbier one by the

---

[1] promenade—public place designed for walking, such as a park.

[2] monastery—church building inhabited by monks.

waist, and made her get into one of the cars. Right away she started to bump and scream and forget all about the argument. Since the seat was very narrow, I put my arm around her shoulders, and she didn't say a thing. The other one, who was much slimmer, was riding by herself in another car and seemed to be having a good time. I realized I should have picked her; but it was too late for that, and all I could do was look at her from my car while she laughed to herself, showing her small teeth, whenever she crashed into another car. With one such jolt a strand of her long hair got into her mouth, and that seemed to make her choke with laughter. A boy tried to climb into her car; but she pushed him away rather violently, suddenly turning serious. That's when I saw, before she drove off again, that she was prettier than she'd seemed at first glance.

I get seasick easily, so I didn't ride on the flying saucers when they took it into their heads to go; and I stood there watching them while they whirled through the air, screaming with fright, holding down their skirts, clutching the chain so as not to fall off. A boy started to scare them by violently rocking back and forth against the chain while it was whirling at top speed, and it looked as though his seat would come loose and throw him into the bay.

Everything was going just fine; but when I invited them to come sit in the park, in the dark part, they said they had to go. I insisted it was still early and that we ought to rest a while in the park, but all I could get from them was a promise they'd come back tonight.

After they left, so as not to go straight home, I sat down on a low stone wall behind Padre Varela. The benches were full of lovers frantically fondling each other. I heard the sound of scissors behind me. An old woman surrounded by bags and wrapping paper was cutting up bread and throwing it to a dog. They seemed to be all set to spend the night. I tried to get a good look at the old woman. It was very hard to do in the dark. She was sitting with her back to the carnival. When the pieces of bread stopped coming, the dog lay down among the bundles. The old woman looked inside the bag closest to her but couldn't quite make up her mind to take anything out. She spent a long time like that. Then she wrapped herself in a burlap sack, clutched her legs, and rested her head on her knees. It occurred to me I ought to give her some money so she could get something to eat. I toyed with the idea for a while but I couldn't make up my mind to do anything.

Tonight I'll have to get to the park early.

Tuesday

What luck! The girl came, the slimmer one. Very late, but she did come. Another one came with her, not as young and not as pretty either. I'd waited a long time, walking up and down in front of the carnival. I tried to remember whether I'd said I'd meet them over there or in the park or at the wall by the Avenida del Puerto. When it seemed they weren't going to come anymore I sat down on the dark side, where the lovers sit. It was Monday, so hardly anybody was there. I'd come very early. Behind me, in the same place as the night before last, I saw the old woman from Sunday, but without the dog. She was slowly eating something greasy and wrapped in newspaper that she pulled out with her dirty fingers. It took her forever to swallow each mouthful. I had to look away. I noticed that her hair isn't white but yellow, maybe from the soil of the park.

After a bit Ester and her friend arrived. I thought we could go on all the carnival rides since they were empty and there was nobody to bother us. Ester said no, that we should sit down on a bench on the other sidewalk, the one that's lit, and anyhow she had to leave in a minute. I paid no attention. Women always say they've got to leave as soon as they show up for a date. Over where we sat down, a street light shone right in my face, while she was partly hidden in the shadows. And I wanted so badly to see her in the light and close up! (This morning, for example, I couldn't form any clear mental picture of her.) The light bothered my eyes but I didn't want to suggest moving. That might have got her telling me again that she had to go. Pretty soon her friend said she wanted to look at the ships on the bay and left.

Then I could see that Ester isn't pretty in a straightforward and ordinary sense, but in some vague, almost subtle, way. There's a touch of **mockery**[3] in her eyes, but I suppose that's because I started right in to tell her, without stopping, everything that was going through my head. Whenever I did pause to let her say something, she just kept quiet. She's given to watching people and laughing with a show of her teeth. I asked her to meet me again, there or anyplace she wanted, in her house if she liked. She doesn't seem like the kind of girl that hangs out in a park, even though she's come to meet me like this, without knowing me and so late at night. All this time I couldn't take my eyes off her. Her skin is so delicate. I think of all her skin, tight and delicate under the dress that hugs her thighs and forces her to walk with short little steps.

Wednesday

Last night she didn't come. Maybe because it was drizzling. It would drizzle and clear up and then about nine it turned to a steady drizzle. By then I knew she wasn't coming, but just the same I kept dragging myself around the park getting wet. The carnival was closed. I walked up and down the streets that run into the avenue.

---

[3] **mockery**—ridicule; scorn.

I went down Cuarteles, as always, and then up Peña Pobre, hoping to run into her, though I avoid going there since they tore down almost the whole block to build one of those awful "parking facilities." I didn't see her. I was tired and went back to the park and sat down on the wall where I was sitting Sunday, the day we met. I don't know why I felt so worn out and still feel that way today. I haven't been able to do a thing. As though I'd walked all over Havana.

Thursday

It's a good thing Ester came last night. She showed up alone. Actually I didn't want her to come. You start attaching importance to these things, and they get blown up out of all proportion.

That's what I told her last night, laughing, when we met. As always she kept looking at me and seemed to be having a good time. We had to talk about *something.* I talk to her constantly just so she won't leave right away. She laughs and looks at me. What might she be thinking about when she's looking at me? We were sitting on the bench she always insists on, under the street light. After a little argument that she always wins, I go along with her, although the light bothers my eyes. Today, for example, I've had to wash with *vicaria* water just to write these lines in my notebook. I don't believe in these things, but my cleaning woman is always singing the praises of *vicaria* and sets a bowl of the water out for me overnight so I'll wash with it before starting to write. And so as not to argue with her I wash myself, because I know she's watching me.

Ester didn't stay long. I suspect somebody doesn't want her to come. That's the only explanation for her being so **reserved.**[4]

---

[4] **reserved**—shy.

Friday

. . . how pretty she is! Last night I could really see her in the coffee shop. She finally let me buy her a cup of coffee. I was coming through the park and saw her waiting for me on the corner. Maybe she wasn't waiting for me and had just come for a little fresh air; but for some reason it seemed to me that, yes, she was waiting for me. Everybody was looking at her and I couldn't help showing my annoyance, because after all she was with me. Her hands are small. She chews her nails and hides her hands from me so I won't notice, and I pretend I don't. Last night I told her she has very pretty hands, and right away she hid them against the seat, under her thighs. The skin of her arm is very delicate. The light shone on the brown hair that rises in waves from her forehead and that she's constantly patting down. How I'd like to run my fingers through her hair! Last night I noticed something in her that I hadn't noticed before, something extraordinary. She has some delicate little moles on her forehead; the smallest one is on her temple, almost hidden by her hair. She really has a beautiful forehead. Now I'm recalling her lips, always half open with a little mocking expression. Last night, maybe because of the heat, she was wearing a dress cut low under the arms that showed a bit of her breasts. I'm trying to remember what we talked about last night, and I can't. I was relieved she was there. I'd been so afraid she wouldn't come. A few minutes before she got up to leave, I put my hand on her shoulder. She quickly drew back. All I told her when we said good night was that I'd be there waiting for her. I can't say how long we talked.

On my way home I saw the old woman with the dog, sleeping on the sidewalk. It was very late. It had started to drizzle. The drizzle must have awakened her. She came over toward where I was, under the tree, and threw a blanket over her head. She gave off a sickening

stench.[5] Other shapes that had been sleeping on the grass and that I hadn't seen also got up. I saw them looking for shelter under pieces of newspaper or bags. The headlights of a bus hit the old woman. Her skin is blackish and wrinkled. Her body is a mass of bones covered with burlap sacks and rags. I've never seen such an old face. The dirt on her face has hardened as the sweat and the rain have dried, and her wrinkles have grown rigid. It's depressing to see a sort of homeless shelter like that, hidden among the trees.

Sunday

Last night I didn't see Ester. But the worst of it is that maybe she was close by and I couldn't see her. Though come to think of it, even if I didn't see her, she was bound to see me. In the afternoon I decided to buy some dark glasses. I never go out in the afternoon because it's so hot, and I spend the time reading or writing; but I realized I had to wear dark glasses so the irritation of my eyes wouldn't be so obvious. In the mirror I could see the glasses looked good on me. Maybe Ester will like the change. But it was so dark that now I'm not sure whether she came, because I had trouble making things out. I ran after two women who I thought looked like her but weren't. I decided to wait for her without leaving my spot.

The old woman was in the park again, in her usual place. As I watched her, and just to pass the time, I started to wonder what dirty miserable people like that might live off. When she's with others, they never talk to each other. The others laugh or talk to themselves as she does, or dig through their bundles in search of something. While I was watching her she spread a newspaper on the grass and lay down to sleep.

---

[5] **stench**—strong smell.

Tuesday

I saw Ester last night. I wish I'd never seen her! Sunday night she didn't come. I waited two hours in the usual place. The old woman picked that time to hang her clothes on the trees because it had rained and everything was soaked. She came over to me to ask for a cigarette and I quickly changed places to avoid her, but I didn't go far. I thought Ester might be looking for me from a way off and if she didn't see me she might leave. But it seems she didn't come. I stayed in the park very late. I'm sure, positive, that she didn't come.

Last night I left home early because I thought I might have to spend a long time looking for her. I kept walking around, in hopes of seeing her come out of some place. I went down Cuarteles, exhausted, and I saw her. She was with her friend from the first night, who didn't recognize me. They were heading for the park, though not by themselves but with two boys. The younger one had his arm around Ester's waist. Ester was wearing the same tight dress as on the first day, the one that clings to her thighs.

Thursday

Last night I got ready to go out; but at the last minute, when I was all set, I decided to stay home. The weather isn't good; and besides, I've been going out too much recently. I don't feel quite well.

Saturday

I stayed away from the park Thursday, and last night, too. The weather was still bad. It's gotten to where it's raining every night, and it's so humid it's not healthy for anybody. Yesterday afternoon I felt better and eventually went out, because I was tired of staying home. I realized I ought to go to the barber. That always makes me feel better. That barber's always trying to push some product or other, some brilliantine,[6] some hair dye; and this time he wound up making a sale. I'm in no mood for arguing these days. He didn't just sell me something, he demonstrated it for me. By the time I realized what was going on he'd dyed my hair with a **patented**[7] German product, he says, and because the dark hair goes better with the dark glasses. If I don't like it, it wears off in a few days. Maybe he's right. At least you get to change the same old way you look. And while he was at it, he went on to sell me an eyebrow pencil, according to him so the eyebrows won't clash with the glasses or the dark hair. I wound up buying it all, I was getting that eager to get out of there.

Before going to bed I went out again. I dropped by the park, quickly, without looking much, because I was sure Ester wouldn't come and I didn't want to build up any false hopes. I stopped a moment in the coffee shop and had a cup of coffee. Just to buy something more I bought a pack of cigarettes, which is something I never do because I don't smoke. After I bought it I wondered what I'd do with it. Suddenly I thought I could give it to the old woman, who'd asked me for a cigarette the other night. I crossed the street and saw her in her usual spot. I came up without her seeing me. She was sleeping. I sat down near her for a bit to see what she was doing. Sitting on the grass so I could see her better, I spent a long time observing her carefully. I shouted to see whether she'd wake up. Gradually she came to. When she saw the cigarettes she grabbed for the package. There was something so **sordid**[8] about her that I decided not to let her have it. I put it in my pocket and went home. Sordid, that's the right word for it, sordid.

---

[6] brilliantine—hair oil.

[7] **patented**—unique; invented.

[8] **sordid**—dirty; miserable.

Sunday

Something terrible has happened. I wish I'd never met Ester. Last night I saw her again in the park. I think it was the worst night of my life. I haven't been able to sleep. I sent away the cleaning woman because I don't want her to see me like this. Besides, she pokes her nose into everything. Ester and I were together a little over half an hour. When I got to the park she was sitting there; and she greeted me as though nothing had happened, as though we'd seen each other the night before. I couldn't think of what to say. I sat down next to her. It was very noisy because they'd started up the carnival, and those loudspeakers make a dreadful racket. I had to repeat and shout what I was saying. At one point she brought her ear closer to me so as to hear. She was laughing because it seems I was blowing in her ear as I talked and that made her laugh. Her ear brushed against my mouth. Her ear is covered with an almost invisible down. The music stopped but I was telling her something and although there wasn't any music anymore I kept on talking into her ear. All I remember is that I kissed her on the neck and under her arm and that what happened afterward was awful. I think Ester stood up suddenly, because I fell to the ground. People started to gather around us, those people who are everyplace and don't have anything to do. I heard her screaming and saying terrible things to me, but I can't remember what they were. All I know is that last night was the most horrible night of my whole life.

Monday

Last night I sat in the usual place. I wasn't expecting anything, but since that's better than staying home I wound up going to the same old place. Very late, it was almost morning, I walked along the streets, stopping in front of many houses. It was so quiet you could hear the breathing of people sleeping next to the windows. Maybe Ester sleeps next to the window. It's so hot. Maybe she sleeps naked to take advantage of every little breeze. I looked in a window and tried to pierce the darkness. Maybe she sleeps next to the window. Maybe she sleeps naked. I am very tired.

Tuesday

My most serious mistake was not to give her my address. If I'd given her my address maybe she'd try to see me, but I didn't. That was my worst mistake. What if somebody knocked at the door in the middle of all this silence . . . She didn't come last night, either. Though I knew she wouldn't come, because there was a heavy drizzle, I sat for a while in the usual spot, covering myself with newspapers.

Thursday

I think the old woman is sick. Last night I sat near her a long time. She didn't budge. She was sitting propped up against a tree, with her eyes closed and her head leaning back against the trunk of the tree, which isn't her usual position. I've noticed that when she dozes off her chin always sinks onto her chest, with the body leaning forward, and her head comes down to rest on her knees.

Last night spit was dribbling from her mouth. Maybe she's dying or close to it. But then, when you reach that state you're no good to anybody. I was there almost through the early morning hours. Anyhow, it's hard for me to be at home.

Friday

Something extraordinary happened to me this morning. I woke up in the park. All night long, in my mind I was going over every moment of my life. I must have fallen asleep. There are a lot of hours in a night, and I can't have spent them all thinking. The trees started to turn blue and then green. It got lighter. At that point I know I fell asleep. When I opened my eyes the sun was shining on my face. All night long I'd been hungry. When I woke up I'd got over it. I came home because the sun was beating down on me and went to bed without breakfast. Ester and I bathed naked in the waters of a spring. Since it was night, the mad perfume of the ilang-ilang tree rose from the depths of the forest.

Sunday

Ester hasn't come, but I'm sure she will. The trouble would be if she came looking for me and didn't find me. Or if she came very late one night. I'm so hungry I can't think straight. The old woman gave me something to eat and some newspapers with which to cover myself. I fell asleep in spite of all that racket that comes from the carnival and all those crowds of people. Tonight I'll have to bring something to eat.

QUESTIONS TO CONSIDER

1. What picture do you get of the park in which the narrator meets Ester? What kind of a neighborhood does it seem to be?

2. Why do you think the narrator can never remember exactly what Ester says to him, even when she screams at him?

3. How does the narrator's reaction to the homeless person reflect on his own character?

4. What is ironic in the narrator's description of people in the park as "people who are everyplace and don't have anything to do"? What other ironies can you find in the story?

5. Why do you think the author gives the reader so little information about the characters?

The Tree

BY MARÍA LUISA BOMBAL

Translated by Richard Cunningham and Lucía Guerra

María Luisa Bombal (Chile, 1910–1980) was considered one of Chile's national treasures. She lived much of her life in other countries, spending her adolescent years in Paris before moving to Argentina in 1931. There she associated with and gained the admiration of the writers for the famous magazine Sur. One of the magazine's founders, Jorge Luis Borges, was a devoted fan. Much of Bombal's work has underlying feminist themes, as Shrouded Woman, House of Mist, and "The Tree" so clearly demonstrate. In this particular story, a naive woman gains self-awareness after years of living in the shadow of others.

The pianist sits down, coughs from force of habit and concentrates for a moment. The clusters of lights illuminating the hall gradually dim until they glow like dying embers, whereupon a musical phrase rises in the

silence, swells: clear, sharp and judiciously **capricious.**[1]
Mozart, maybe, Brígida thinks to herself. As usual, she
has forgotten to ask for the program. Mozart—or perhaps Scarlatti . . . She knew so little about music! And it
was not because she lacked an ear or the inclination. On
the contrary, as a child it had been she who demanded
piano lessons; no one needed to impose them on her, as
was the case with her sisters. Today, however, her
sisters could sight-read perfectly, while she . . . she had
abandoned her studies after the first year. The reason for
the **inconstancy**[2] was as simple as it was shameful: she
had never been able, never, to learn the key of F. "I don't
understand—my memory serves me only to the key of
C." And her father's indignation! "Would that I could
lay down this burden: a miserable widower with children
to educate! My poor Carmen! How she would have
suffered with such a daughter! The creature is retarded!"

Brígida was the youngest of six girls—all endowed
with different temperaments. She received little attention
from her father because dealing with the other five
daughters reduced him to such a perplexed and worn-
out state that he preferred to ease his burden by insisting
on her **feeblemindedness.**[3] "I won't struggle any
longer—it's useless. Leave her alone. If she chooses not
to study, so be it. If she would rather spend her time in
the kitchen listening to ghost stories, that's fine with me.
If she favors playing with dolls at the age of sixteen,
let her play." And so Brígida had kept to her dolls,
remaining almost totally ignorant as far as formal
education was concerned.

How pleasant it is to be ignorant! Not to know
exactly who Mozart was—to ignore his origins, his
influences, the particularities of his technique! To simply
let oneself be led by the hand, as now. . . .

[1] **capricious**—unexpected.
[2] **inconstancy**—ever changing ways.
[3] **feeblemindedness**—stupidity.

For in truth Mozart leads her—transporting her onto a bridge suspended above crystal water running over a bed of pink sand. She is dressed in white, tilting on one shoulder an open parasol of Chantilly lace, elaborate and fine as a spider's web.

"You look younger every day, Brígida. Yesterday I ran into your husband—I mean your ex-husband. His hair is now completely white."

But she makes no reply, unwilling to tarry[4] while crossing the bridge Mozart has fabricated toward the garden of her youth.

Tall blossoming spouts in which the water sings. Her eighteen years; her chestnut braids that, unbound, **cascaded**[5] to her waist; her golden complexion; her dark eyes so wide and questioning. A small mouth with full lips; a sweet smile; and the lightest, most gracious body in the world. Of what was she thinking, seated by the fountain's edge? Of nothing. "She is as silly as she is pretty," they used to say. But she did not mind being silly, nor acting the dunce at parties. One by one, her sisters received proposals of marriage. No one asked her.

Mozart! Now he conducts her to a blue marble staircase on which she descends between two rows of ice lilies. And now he opens a wrought-iron gate of spikes with golden tips so that she may throw herself on Luis, her father's intimate friend. From childhood, she would run to Luis when everyone else abandoned her. He would pick her up and she would encircle his neck between giggles that were like tiny bird cries; she would fling kisses like disorderly raindrops on his eyes, his forehead and his hair—which even then was graying (had he never been young?). "You are a necklace," Luis would say. "You are like a necklace of sparrows."

---

[4] tarry—linger in one place.

[5] **cascaded**—fell.

That is why she had married him. Because at the side of that solemn and **taciturn**[6] man she felt less guilty for being what she was: foolish, playful and indolent. Yes—now, after so many years, she realizes that she had not married Luis for love; yet she cannot put her finger on why, why she left him so suddenly one day.

But at this moment Mozart takes her nervously by the hand, drawing her into a rhythm second by second more urgent—compelling her to retrace her steps across the garden and onto the bridge at a pace that is almost like fleeing. And after stripping her of the parasol[7] and the transparent crinoline,[8] he closes the door on her past with a note at once firm and sweet—leaving her in the concert hall, dressed in black, applauding mechanically as the artificial lights rekindle their flame.

* * *

Again shadows, and the prelude of silence.

And now Beethoven begins to stir the lukewarm tide of his notes beneath a summer moon. How far the sea has retreated! Brígida walks seaward, down the beach toward the distant, bright, smooth water; but all at once the sea rises, flowing placidly to meet and envelop her—the gentle waves pushing at her back until they press her cheek against the body of a man. And then the waves recede, leaving her stranded on Luis's chest.

"You have no heart, you have no heart," she used to say to him. His heartbeat was so faint that she could not hear it except in rare and unexpected moments. "You are never with me when you are by my side," she would protest in their bedroom when, before going to sleep, he would **ritually**[9] open the evening paper. "Why did you marry me?"

---

[6] **taciturn**—silent and grim.

[7] parasol—small umbrella carried as protection from the sun.

[8] crinoline—coarse, stiff fabric used to line clothing and hats.

[9] **ritually**—according to routine; ceremonially.

"Because you have the eyes of a startled fawn," he would reply, giving her a kiss. And she, abruptly cheerful, would proudly accept the weight of his gray head on her shoulder. Oh, that silvery, radiant hair!

"Luis, you have never told me exactly what color your hair was when you were a boy. Or how your mother felt when you began going gray at the age of fifteen. What did she say? Did she laugh? Cry? And you—were you proud or ashamed? And at school— what did your classmates say? Tell me, Luis, tell me. . . ."

"Tomorrow. I am sleepy, Brígida. Very tired. Turn off the light."

Unconsciously, he would turn away from her in sleep; just as she unconsciously sought her husband's shoulder all night long, searching for his breath, groping blindly for protection as an enclosed and thirsty plant bends its tendrils[10] toward warmth and moisture.

In the mornings, when the maid would open the Venetian blinds, Luis was no longer next to her. He had departed quietly without so much as a salutation, for fear the necklace of sparrows would fasten **obstinately**[11] around his neck. "Five minutes, five minutes, no more. Your office will not disappear if you are five minutes late, Luis."

Her awakenings. Ah, how sad her awakenings! But— it was curious—no sooner had she entered her **boudoir**[12] than the sadness vanished as if by an enchantment.

Waves crash, clashing far away, murmuring like a sea of leaves. Beethoven? No.

It is the tree outside her dressing-room window. She had only to enter the room to experience an almost overpowering sense of well-being.

How hot the bedroom always was in the morning! And what harsh light! By contrast, in the dressing-room

---

[10] tendrils—slender coils.

[11] **obstinately**—stubbornly.

[12] **boudoir**—dressing room.

even her eyes felt rested, refreshed. The faded cretonne[13] curtains; the tree casting shadows that undulated on the walls like cold, moving water; the mirrors refracting[14] foliage, creating the illusion of a green and infinite forest. How enjoyable that room was! It seemed a world submerged in an aquarium. And how that huge rubber tree chattered! All the birds in the neighborhood took refuge in it. It was the only tree on that narrow, falling street that sloped from one side of the city directly to the river.

"I am busy. I can't be with you . . . Lots of work to do, I won't be home for lunch . . . Hello . . . yes, I am at the club. An engagement. Eat and go to bed . . . No. I don't know. Better not wait for me, Brígida."

"If I only had friends!" she would sigh. But she bored everyone. "If I tried to be a little less foolish! Yet how does one recover so much lost ground at a single stroke? To be intelligent, you must start very young—isn't that true?"

Her sisters' husbands took them everywhere, but Luis—why had she denied it to herself?—had been ashamed of her, of her ignorance, her shyness, even of her eighteen years. Had he not urged her to pretend that she was at least twenty-one, as though her youth were an embarrassing secret they alone shared?

And at night—he always came to bed so weary! Never paying full attention to what she said. He smiled, yes—a mechanical smile. His caresses were plentiful, but bestowed absentmindedly. Why had he married her? To continue their acquaintance, perhaps simply to put the crowning touch his old friendship with her father.

Maybe life for men was based on a series of established and continuous customs. **Rupturing**[15] this

---

[13] cretonne—upholstery fabric.

[14] refracting—altering the appearance of.

[15] **Rupturing**—breaking.

chain would probably produce disorder, chaos. And after, men would stumble through the streets of the city, roosting[16] on park benches, growing shabbier and more unshaven with each passing day. Luis's life, therefore, was patterned on keeping occupied every minute of the day. Why had she failed to see this sooner? Her father had been right: she was retarded.

"I would like to see snow sometime, Luis."

"This summer I will take you to Europe, and since it will be winter there, you shall have your snow."

"I am quite aware that winter in Europe coincides with our summer. I am not that stupid!"

At times, to rouse him to the rapture of true love, she would throw herself on him and cover him with kisses: weeping, calling, "Luis, Luis, Luis. . . ."

"What? What is the matter? What do you want?"

"Nothing."

"Why do you cry out my name like that, then?"

"No reason. To say your name. I like to say your name."

And he would smile **benevolently,**[17] pleased with the new game.

Summer came—her first summer as a married woman. Several new business ventures forced Luis to postpone the promised European trip.

"Brígida, the heat will be terrible in Buenos Aires shortly. Why don't you spend the summer on your father's ranch?"

"Alone?"

"I would visit you every week, from Saturday to Monday."

She sat down on the bed, **primed**[18] to insult him. But she could not find the hurting words. She knew nothing, nothing—not even how to offend.

---

[16] roosting—resting.

[17] **benevolently**—kindly.

[18] **primed**—prepared.

"What is wrong with you? What are you thinking of, Brígida?"

He was leaning over her, worried, for the first time in their marriage and unconcerned about violating his customary punctuality at the office.

"I am sleepy," Brígida had replied childishly, hiding her face in the pillow.

For once, he rang her up at lunchtime from his club. But she had refused to come to the phone, angrily wielding a weapon she had discovered without thinking: silence.

That same evening she dined across from him with lowered eyes and nerves strung tight.

"Are you still angry, Brígida?"

But she did not answer.

"You know perfectly well that I love you. But I can't be with you all the time. I am a very busy man. When you reach my age, you become a slave to a thousand obligations."

"Shall we go out tonight?"

"No? Very well, I will be patient. Tell me, did Roberto call from Montevideo?"

"What a lovely dress! Is it new?"

"Is it new, Brígida? Answer me. Say something."

But she refused to break her silence.

And then the unexpected, the astonishing, the absurd. Luis rises from his chair and slaps his napkin on the table, slamming the door as he stomps from the house.

She, too, had gotten to her feet, stunned, trembling with indignation at such injustice. "And I . . . and I . . ." she stammered, "I, who for almost an entire year . . . when for the first time I take the liberty of lodging a complaint . . . ah, I am leaving—I am leaving this very night! I shall never set foot in this house again . . ." And she jerked open the **armoires**[19] in her dressing room, strewing clothes furiously in all directions. It was then that she heard a banging against the windowpane.

She ran to the window and opened it, not knowing how or from where the courage came. It was the rubber tree, set in motion by the storm, knocking its branches on the glass as though calling her to witness how it twisted and **contorted**[20] like a fierce black flame under the burning sky of that summer night.

Heavy rain soon began to lash its cold leaves. How lovely! All night long she could hear the rain thrashing, splashing through the leaves of the rubber tree like a thousand tiny rivers sliding down imaginary canals. All night long she heard the ancient trunk creak and moan, the storm raging outside while she curled into a ball between the sheets of the wide bed, very close to Luis.

Handfuls of pearls raining on a silver roof. Chopin. Etudes[21] by Frédéric Chopin.

How many mornings had she awakened as soon as she sensed that her husband, now likewise maintaining an obstinate silence, had slipped from bed?

Her dressing room: the window thrown wide, the odor of river and grass floating in that hospitable chamber, and the mirrors wearing a veil of fog.

Chopin intermingles in her **turbulent**[22] memory with rain hissing through the leaves of the rubber tree like some hidden waterfall—so **palpable**[23] that even the roses on the curtains seem moist.

What to do in summer when it rains so often? Spend the day in her room feigning sadness, a **convalescence**?[24] One afternoon Luis had entered timidly. Had sat down stiffly. There was a long silence.

---

[19] **armoires**—large clothes cabinets.

[20] **contorted**—changed shape.

[21] Etudes—musical compositions.

[22] **turbulent**—chaotic; disorderly.

[23] **palpable**—touchable.

[24] **convalescence**—period of getting well; recuperating from illness.

"Then it is true, Brígida? You no longer love me?"

A sudden joy seized her. She might have shouted, "No, no. I love you Luis, I love you," if he had given her time, if he had not almost immediately added, with his habitual calm, "In any case, I do not think it would be convenient for us to separate, Brígida. Such a move requires much thought."

Her impulse sank as fast as it had surfaced. What was the use of exciting herself! Luis loved her tenderly, with moderation; if he ever came to hate her, it would be a just and prudent hatred. And that was life. She walked to the window and placed her forehead against the cold glass. There was the rubber tree, serenely accepting the pelting rain. The room was fixed in shadow, quiet and ordered. Everything seemed to be held in an eternal and very noble **equilibrium**.[25] That was life. And there was a certain **grandeur**[26] in accepting it thus: mediocre, like something definite and **irremediable**.[27] While underneath it all there seemed to rise a melody of grave and slow words that **transfixed**[28] her: "Always. Never. . . . "

And in this way the hours, days and years pass. Always! Never! Life! Life!

Collecting herself, she realized that her husband had stolen from the room.

"Always! Never! . . ." And the rain, secret and steady, still whispered in Chopin.

* * *

Summer stripped the leaves from its burning calendar. Luminous and blinding pages fell like golden

---

[25] **equilibrium**—balance.

[26] **grandeur**—greatness; feeling of being good.

[27] **irremediable**—hopeless; irreparable.

[28] **transfixed**—amazed.

swords; pages also of malignant dampness like breeze from a swamp; pages of furious and brief storms, of hot wind—the wind that carries the "carnation of the air" and hangs it on the huge rubber tree.

Some children used to play hide-and-seek among the enormous, twisted roots that pushed up the paving stones on the sidewalk, and the tree overflowed with laughter and whispering. On those days she would look from the window and clap her hands; but the children **dispersed**[29] in fear, without noticing the childlike smile of a girl who wanted to join the game.

Alone, she would lean on her elbows at the window for a long time, watching the foliage swaying—a breeze blew along that street which sloped directly to the river—and it was like staring deep into moving water or the dancing flames in a fireplace. One could kill time in this fashion, no need for thought made foolish by peace of mind.

She lit the first lamp just as the room began to fill with twilight smoke, and the first lamp flickered in the mirrors, multiplying like fireflies eager to hasten the night.

And night after night she dozed beside her husband, suffering at **intervals**.[30] But when her pain tightened so that it pierced like a knife thrust, when she was besieged by the desire to wake Luis—to hit him or caress him— she tiptoed to her dressing room and opened the window. Immediately the room came alive with discreet sounds and discreet presences, with mysterious footsteps, the fluttering of wings, the sudden rustling of vegetation, the soft chirping of a cricket perched on the bark of the rubber tree under the stars of a hot summer night.

---

[29] **dispersed**—scattered.

[30] **intervals**—from time to time; on and off.

Little by little her fever went down as her bare feet grew cold on the reed mat. She did not know why it was so easy to suffer in that room.

* * *

Chopin's melancholy stringing of one Etude after another, stringing of one melancholy after another, **imperturbably**.[31]

And autumn came. The dry leaves hovered an instant before settling on the grass of the narrow garden, on the sidewalk of that sloping street. The leaves came loose and fell . . . The top of the rubber tree remained green but underneath it turned red, darkened like the worn-out lining of a **sumptuous**[32] evening cape. And now the room seemed to be submerged in a goblet of dull gold.

Lying on the divan,[33] she waited patiently for the dinner hour and the improbable arrival of Luis. She had resumed speaking to him, had become his again without enthusiasm or anger. She no longer loved him. But she no longer suffered. On the contrary, an unexpected feeling of fulfillment and **placidity**[34] had taken hold of her. Nothing, no one could hurt her now. It may be that true happiness lies in the conviction that one has irrevocably lost happiness. It is only then that we can begin to live without hope or fear, able finally to enjoy all the small pleasures, which are the most lasting.

A thunderous noise, followed by a flash of light from which she **recoils**,[35] shaking.

The intermission? No. The rubber tree.

---

[31] **imperturbably**—calmly and without interruption.

[32] **sumptuous**—fancy.

[33] divan—long, backless sofa.

[34] **placidity**—calmness; tranquility.

[35] **recoils**—shrinks back in fear.

Having started to work early in the morning without her knowledge, they had felled it with a single stroke of the axe. "The roots were breaking up the sidewalk and, naturally, the neighborhood committee. . . ."

Dazed, she has shielded her eyes with her hands. When she recovers her sight, she stands and looks around. What does she see?

The concert hall suddenly ablaze with light, the audience filing out?

No. She is imprisoned in the web of her past, trapped in the dressing room—which has been invaded by a terrifying white light. It was as if they had ripped off the roof; a crude light entering from every direction, seeping through her very pores, burning her with its coldness. And she saw everything bathed in that cold light: Luis, his wrinkled face, his hands crisscrossed with ropy discolored veins and the gaudy cretonnes.

Frightened, she runs to the window. The window now opens directly on a narrow street, so narrow that her room almost brushes against a shiny skyscraper. On the ground floor, shop windows and more shop windows, full of bottles. At the corner, a row of automobiles lined up in front of a service station painted red. Some boys in their shirtsleeves are kicking a ball in the middle of the street.

And all that ugliness lay embedded in her mirrors, along with nickel-plated balconies, shabby clotheslines and canary cages.

They had stolen her intimacy, her secret; she found herself naked in the middle of the street, naked before an old husband who turned his back on her in bed, who had given her no children. She does not understand why, until then, she had not wanted children, how she had resigned herself to the idea of a life without children. Nor does she comprehend how for a whole year she had tolerated Luis's laughter, that overcheerful laughter, that false laughter of a man who has trained himself in joviality because it is necessary to laugh on certain occasions.

Lies! Her resignation and serenity were lies; she wanted love, yes, love, and trips and madness and love, love. . . .

"But, Brígida . . . why are you leaving? Why did you stay so long?" Luis had asked. Now she would have to know how to answer him.

"The tree, Luis, the tree! They have cut down the rubber tree."

QUESTIONS TO CONSIDER

1. How does the concert affect Brígida?

2. What kind of relationship exists between Brígida and her family? Between Brígida and her husband? Between Brígida and the world outside her window?

3. In what ways do you think Brígida's dissatisfaction with her husband is justified?

4. Besides the street outside, what do you think is revealed to Brígida when the rubber tree is cut down?

Literary Atlas

Mexico

Rosario Castellanos
Sor Juana Inés de la Cruz
Octavio Paz
Elena Poniatowska
Juan Rulfo
Ilan Stavans

Guatemala

Augusto Monterroso
Alcina Lubitch Domecq

Mexico, Central America, and the Caribbean

Sor Juana Inés
de la Cruz

Ilan Stavans

Juan Rulfo

Octavio Paz

Belize

**Dominican
Republic**

Jamaica

Haiti

Puerto Rico

Cuba

Calvert Casey

Honduras

Nicaragua

Panama

El Salvador

Costa Rica

Colombia

Gabriel García Márquez

Ecuador

South America

Peru

Gabriel García
Márquez

Pablo Neruda

Isabel Allende

Gabriela Mistral

Chile

Isabel Allende
María Luisa Bombal
Gabriela Mistral
Pablo Neruda

Venezuala

Guyana

Suriname

French Guiana

Bolivia

Paraguay

Brazil

Nélida Piñón

João Guimarães Rosa

Clarice Lispector

Jorge Luis Borges

Argentina

Jorge Luis Borges

Julio Cortázar

Domingo Faustino Sarmiento

Uruguay

Horatio Quiroga

The Human
Landscape

from

Facundo

BY DOMINGO FAUSTINO SARMIENTO

Translated by Stuart Edgar Grummon

*Domingo Faustino Sarmiento (Argentina, 1811–1888) is one of
the first Latin American writers to participate in politics, ruling as
president of Argentina between 1868 and 1874. He greatly
admired the United States political system and condemned the
tyrannical regime of Argentina's former dictator, Juan Manuel de
Rosas. Sarmiento's most famous novel,* Facundo, *is a powerful
critique of nondemocratic institutions and of the type of repression
perpetrated during Rosas's reign. Here Sarmiento discusses the
country of Argentina and the need to civilize its people.*

"So vast is the extent of the pampas[1] that, in the north, they are bounded by palm groves and, in the south, by the eternal snows."

The American continent ends at the south in a point, at the extremity of which are the Straits of Magellan. To the west, at a short distance from the Pacific, the Chilean Andes run parallel to the coast. The land that lies to the east of that mountain chain and west of the Atlantic, following the Plate River into the interior along the Uruguay and beyond, is the territory known as the United Provinces of the Río de la Plata in which blood is still being shed to change its name to the Argentine Republic or Argentine Confederation. To the north are Paraguay and Bolivia, its presumed limits.

The immense extent of land that lies at its remote borders is altogether uninhabited and possesses **navigable**[2] rivers that have not yet been traveled even by the frail canoe. The ailment that afflicts the Argentine Republic is size. The desert surrounds it on every side and penetrates to its very heart. In general, wastes, devoid of human dwellings, are the **incontestable**[3] boundaries between the provinces. In Argentina there is immensity on every hand: the plains are immense, the forests immense, the rivers immense, and the horizon always uncertain, the earth forever receding into the cloud formations and haze which prevent one from seeing the exact point in the distance at which the earth ends and the sky begins. To the north and south, savages lie in an ambush, waiting for moonlit nights, to fall like a pack of hyenas on the defenseless settlements and on the cattle grazing in the fields. A solitary caravan of heavy wagons lumbers slowly across the pampas and

---

[1] **pampas**—treeless grassland areas in South America, especially in Argentina.

[2] **navigable**—able to be traveled upon by boat.

[3] **incontestable**—indisputable; unarguable.

halts occasionally to rest. Its crew, gathered around a small fire, automatically turns its gaze toward the south at the slightest breath of wind that rustles the dry grass, to peer into the inky blackness of the night, looking for the sinister hordes of savages who may fall upon them without warning from one moment to the next.

If their ears hear no sound and their eyes are unable to pierce the dark veil covering the still solitude, they glance for complete reassurance at the ears of a horse **picketed**[4] near the fire, to see whether they are pricked up or negligently drooping back. Then the interrupted conversation is resumed, or the traveler carries to his mouth the halfscorched dried beef on which he subsists. If it is not the **proximity**[5] of the Indians that worries the campers, it is the fear of a lurking tiger or of a snake that they may tread on. This habitual and permanent insecurity of life seems to me to stamp upon the Argentine character a certain stoical resignation to violent death which makes even that merely one of the misfortunes inseparable from life—a way of dying like any other. This may perhaps explain in part the indifference with which death is dealt out and received, without leaving any deep or lasting impression upon the survivors.

The inhabited portion of this country, so privileged by nature and embracing all varieties of climates, may be divided into three distinct zones which cause differences of character among the inhabitants, growing out of the necessity of their adapting themselves to their natural environments.

In the north reaching to the Chaco, the impenetrable branches of a dense forest cover areas that would seem incredible but for the fact that nothing **colossal**[6]

---

[4] **picketed**—standing guard.
[5] **proximity**—nearness.
[6] **colossal**—immense.

throughout the whole length and breadth of South America can be considered extraordinary.

In the central zone, lying parallel to the former, the pampa and the forest have long contended with each other for the possession of the soil. In places, the forest prevails, then it dwindles into stunted, thorny thickets, only to become forest again, where some river provides more favorable conditions. At length, in the south, the pampa triumphs, unbounded and unbroken. It is the image of the sea upon the land; it is land as on a map—land yet waiting for the command to bring forth plants and seeds of every kind.

As a noteworthy feature of the physical aspect of this country, we may cite its abundance of navigable rivers which flow eastward from every point of the compass to **converge**[7] in the Río de la Plata. They offer a mighty and worthy tribute to the ocean, which receives them into its waters with visible indications of disturbance and respect. But these immense channels, carved out by the **solicitous**[8] hand of Nature, have wrought no change in national customs. The descendant of the Spanish adventurers who colonized Argentina detests navigation, feeling himself a prisoner within the narrow confines of a boat or launch. When a great river cuts across his path, he calmly removes his clothes, prepares his horse, drives him into the river, and makes him swim for some island visible in the distance. Having reached it, horse and rider rest, and thus, from island to island, the entire crossing is finally accomplished.

So the Argentine gaucho[9] despises the greatest blessing that Providence[10] bestows upon any people, looking upon it rather as an obstacle to his movements than as the most powerful means of facilitating them.

---

[7] **converge**—come together.

[8] **solicitous**—caring.

[9] gaucho—cattleman; cowboy.

[10] Providence—God; superior guiding force.

For this reason, the source of national growth that brought fame to ancient Egypt, glory to Holland, and rapid development to North America—the navigation of rivers and the building of canals—remains a latent force neglected by the inhabitants of the banks of the Bermejo, Pilcomayo, Paraná, Paraguay, and Uruguay Rivers. A few small vessels manned by Italians and adventurers sail upstream from the Río de la Plata, but after ascending a few miles even this traffic practically ceases. The instinct for navigation, possessed to such a remarkable degree by the Saxons of the north, was not bestowed upon the Spaniards. Another spirit is needed to quicken these arteries in which a nation's lifeblood today lies stagnant. Of all rivers which should bring civilization, power, and wealth to the **remotest**[11] interior of the continent and make Santa Fé, Entre Ríos, Corrientes, Córdoba, Salta, Tucumán, and Jujuy, cities overflowing with wealth, population, and culture, only one—the Río de la Plata, which embraces them all— yields rich benefits to those who live on its banks.

At its mouth stand two cities, Montevideo and Buenos Aires, which at present alternately harvest the advantages of their enviable position. Buenos Aires is destined someday to become the most gigantic city of the two Americas. Under a **benignant**[12] climate, mistress of the navigation of a hundred rivers that flow at its feet, reclining luxuriously on an immense territory, and having thirteen provinces in its hinterland with no other outlet for their products, it would have become the American Babylon,[13] if the spirit of the pampas had not blown over it and stifled, at their source, the rich offerings which its rivers and provinces should unceasingly bring. It alone in the whole vast Argentine expanse is in contact with European nations. It alone exploits the

---

[11] **remotest**—farthest away.

[12] **benignant**—agreeable; beneficial.

[13] Babylon—city or place of great luxury, vice, or corruption.

advantages of foreign commerce, and it alone has power and revenues. In vain the provinces have begged it to let a little civilization, industry, and European population trickle through to them. A stupid colonial policy has turned a deaf ear to these appeals, but the provinces took their revenge when they sent Rosas to Buenos Aires—a barbarism of which they have enough and to spare.

Those who used to say: "The Argentine Republic ends at the Arroyo del Medio," have paid dearly for it. Now it stretches from the Andes to the sea, while barbarism and violence have brought Buenos Aires to a lower level than the provinces. We must not complain, however, about Buenos Aires, which is great and is destined to be still greater. We should rather complain to Providence and ask it to alter the **configuration**[14] of the land. This being impossible let us accept as well done what has come from the Creator's hand. Let us rather blame the ignorance of the brutal power that **sterilizes**,[15] for itself and for the provinces, the gifts that nature has lavished upon an erring people. Instead of sending inspiration, wealth, and prosperity to the interior, Buenos Aires now sends it only chains, exterminating hordes, and petty under-tyrants. It also revenges itself for the evil that the provinces inflicted upon it in sending it Rosas!

I have indicated this **monopolistic**[16] position of Buenos Aires to demonstrate that there is such a central-ized and unified organization in Argentina that even had Rosas shouted, "Federation or death!" in good faith, he would have come in the end to the centralized organization which he has today established. We wanted union in civilization and in liberty, however, and have been given only union in barbarism and in slavery! But

---

[14] **configuration**—formation; structure.

[15] **sterilizes**—makes incapable of reproducing.

[16] **monopolistic**—marked by total control; without competitors.

a day will dawn when affairs will take their proper course. What it is now important to understand is that the fruits of civilization are accumulating only in Buenos Aires. The pampas are a very poor **conductor**[17] to carry and distribute them, to provinces. We shall presently see the results of this situation.

But above all these peculiarities of certain parts of our territory, one general, uniform, and constant feature predominates. Whether the land is covered with the gigantic, luxuriant vegetation of the tropics; whether stunted, thorny, waving brakes[18] show that there is a scarcity of lifegiving moisture; or whether, finally, the pampas spread out their unbroken, monotonous surface, the land is generally smooth and level—the sierras[19] of San Luis and Córdoba in the center and a few advanced ramifications of the Andes in the north being scarcely enough to interrupt their boundless continuity. This will be a new element of cohesion for the nation that will one day occupy those vast solitudes, for it is well known that in many countries, mountains and other natural obstacles have maintained the isolation of their inhabitants and preserved their original characteristics.

North America has been destined to become a federation, less because of the original independence of its settlements than because of the length of its Atlantic coastline and the many approaches to the interior afforded by the St. Lawrence in the north, the Mississippi in the south, and the great canal system in the center. The Argentine Republic is "one and indivisible."

---

[17] **conductor**—way, manner.

[18] brakes—thickets.

[19] sierras—rugged mountain ranges.

Many philosophers have held that plains prepare the way for **despotism**,[20] just as mountains offer strongholds for resistance against oppression. The boundless plain which extends from Salta to Buenos Aires and thence to Mendoza, for a distance of more than twenty-one hundred miles, allows our great, heavy wagons to roll unimpeded over roads, to make which the hand of man has scarcely needed to cut down a few scattered trees and thickets. This plain constitutes one of the outstanding features of the interior of the Republic.

To prepare communication routes, the efforts of the individual and the raw state of nature are alone sufficient. If skill would only lend its assistance, however, and if the forces of society were to attempt to supplement the weakness of the individual, the colossal dimensions of the work would make the most enterprising desist and the inadequacy of the effort would make it **inopportune**.[21]

Thus in the matter of roads, savage nature will long **hold sway**,[22] and the influence of civilization will remain weak and ineffective.

Scattered here and there over the limitless expanse which we have described are fourteen provincial capitals, which we would classify according to their geographical position, if we were to list them in their apparent order: Buenos Aires, Santa Fé, Entre Ríos, and Corrientes on the banks of the Paraná; Mendoza, San Juan, Rioja, Catamarca, Tucumán, Salta, and Jujuy, almost in a line parallel to the Chilean Andes; and Santiago, San Luis and Córdoba in the center.

This method of enumerating Argentine provincial capitals, however, does not lead to the social results that I am seeking. The classification which better suits my

---

[20] **despotism**—rule by absolute power.

[21] **inopportune**—inappropriate.

[22] **hold sway**—continue to influence.

purpose is according to the means of livelihood of the country people, for it is this that influences their spirit and character. I have stated above that their proximity to the rivers has had no effect upon them, since the rivers are navigated only to an insignificant extent. At the present time, all of the towns, with the exception of San Juan and Mendoza, live on the products of pasturing. Tucumán also engages in agriculture, and Buenos Aires, in addition to raising millions of head of cattle, devotes itself to the **multifarious**[23] activities of civilized life.

The Argentine cities have the geometrical appearance of almost all South American cities. Their streets are cut at right angles, and their population is widely scattered. One must except Córdoba, however, which, built on a narrow and confined area, has all the appearance of a European city, an effect heightened by the large number of towers and domes of its many splendid churches. The cities are the center of Argentine, Spanish, and European civilization, having art studios, commercial establishments, schools, colleges, courts, and all the **paraphernalia**[24] of cultivated societies.

Elegance of manner, luxury, and European clothes, including the dress coat and frock coat, are at home in the city. I do not make this trivial enumeration idly. The grazing provinces sometimes have no towns at all but their capital cities, and with some of them the open plains end at the city streets. The wilderness encircles them all at a greater or less distance; it constricts and crushes them and savage nature reduces them to narrow oases of civilization set in virgin plains hundreds of square miles in extent, scarcely interrupted by a town or two worthy of the name. Buenos Aires and Córdoba are the two provinces which have been able to establish the greatest

---

[23] **multifarious**—many.

[24] **paraphernalia**—equipment; gear; belongings.

number of nearby towns as supplementary centers of civilization and **municipal**[25] interest—a noteworthy fact.

The city man wears European clothes, and lives the sort of civilized life that we know everywhere. He has laws, ideas of progress, means of instruction, some municipal organization, regular government, etc. When one leaves the confines of the city behind, everything changes in appearance. The country man wears a different costume, which I shall call South American, since it is common to all of our peoples. His way of life and necessities are different, peculiar, and limited. These seem two distinct societies, two alien peoples. Moreover, the country man, far from aspiring to resemble the city dweller, scornfully rejects the latter's luxuries and fine manners, and no city costume, dress coat, cape, saddles, or other European accessory can appear with impunity in the country. Every object of civilized city life is condemned and **proscribed**,[26] and anyone daring to show himself in a frock coat, for example, or riding on an English saddle would draw **derisive**[27] and brutal attacks from the country people.

In the country, lacking all means of civilization and progress—for these can develop only where people are united in large communities—one sees how little the men's education amounts to. Women keep house, cook, shear the sheep, milk the cows, make cheese, and weave the coarse cloth which is made into garments. The woman performs all of the household work and carries on all the domestic industries. Practically all of the work falls to her lot[28] and she is fortunate if one of the menfolk takes the trouble to cultivate a patch of corn for the family table, for bread is not a common article of diet. The children test their strength and for sport learn the

---

[25] **municipal**—metropolitan; civic.

[26] **proscribed**—forbidden; outlawed.

[27] **derisive**—mocking.

[28] lot—responsibility.

use of the lasso and the *boleadoras*[29] with which they keep annoying and **persecuting**[30] the calves and goats. As soon as they have learned to ride, which is generally immediately after they have mastered the art of walking, they do their chores on horseback. Later, as they grow stronger, they range the countryside, taking tumbles and picking themselves up, tripping over rabbit holes, leaping **precipices**,[31] and acquiring skill in horsemanship. At puberty, when they devote themselves to breaking wild colts, death is the punishment that awaits them if their courage or strength should fail for a moment. With their first youth comes complete independence and idleness.

Here begins the gaucho's public life so to speak, for his education is now at an end. One has to see these men, Spaniards only by language and by the confused religious notions which they still retain, in order to understand what haughty and indomitable characters are produced by this struggle of isolated man against savage nature, of reason against brute matter. One must see their heavily bearded faces and expressions as grave as those of Arabs or Asiatics to judge of their pitying disdain for the **sedentary**[32] city man who may have read many books, but cannot throw and kill a wild bull, nor catch a horse alone and on foot in the open country—a man, in short, who has never stopped a tiger, with a dagger in one hand and his poncho wrapped around the other to be thrust into the brute's mouth while the knife pierces his vitals. This habit of surmounting obstacles and of constantly defying and conquering nature develops extraordinarily the gaucho's feeling of individual superiority and self-importance. Argentines of whatever

---

[29] *boleadoras*—short rope, weighted on each end, used to capture running animals.

[30] **persecuting**—treating badly.

[31] **precipices**—cliffs, bluffs.

[32] **sedentary**—inactive; idle.

class, civilized or ignorant, have a high opinion of their own worth as a people. The other American peoples throw this vanity in their faces and act offended at their presumption and arrogance. I believe that the charge is not unwarranted, but I am not concerned about it. God help the people who do not have faith in themselves! Great things have not been wrought for them! How much must the arrogance of these Argentine gauchos, who have seen nothing under the sun better than themselves—not even the wisest or most powerful of men— have contributed to the independence of this part of America? To them, the European is the lowest of the low because he cannot even sit a horse that bucks once or twice. If the origin of this national vanity among the lower classes is petty, the consequences are not for that reason less noble, just as river water is no less pure for having come from a **fetid**,[33] swampy watershed. Their hatred for the educated man is **implacable**[34] and their disgust at his clothes, habits, and manners, insurmountable. Argentine soldiers are moulded out of this clay and it is easy to imagine the **martial**[35] habits of bravery and endurance which such material can develop. It should be added that they are accustomed to killing cattle from infancy and that this necessary act of cruelty at once familiarizes them with the shedding of blood and hardens their hearts against their victims' groans.

Life in the open therefore, has developed physical qualities in the gaucho without any corresponding intellectual ones. His moral character suffers from his habit of mounting the forces of nature and other obstacles. He is strong, proud, and energetic. Uneducated, but without the need for an education, and lacking both a livelihood and necessities, he is happy in his poverty

---

[33] **fetid**—smelly.

[34] **implacable**—inflexible; unbending.

[35] **martial**—having to do with warfare.

and **privations**,[36] which he does not consider as such, never having known comforts or experienced higher desires. Although this disorganization of community life is deep-seated, barbarism resulting from impossibility and futility of moral and intellectual development has none the less its attractive side. The gaucho does not work. His food and clothing are prepared for him at home. His cattle furnish him with both, if he is a landowner, and his employer's or a relative's house, if he is propertyless. The attention required by the cattle is limited to galloping about on horseback and to pleasure **jaunts**.[37] The arrival of branding time, which is like the farmers' harvest, is a festival which is greeted with transports of joy. It is an occasion for every man for sixty miles around to gather and affords an opportunity for a display of incredible skill with the rope. The gaucho approaches the branding ground at the slow, measured pace of his best **courser**,[38] which he reins in while still some distance away. In order to enjoy the spectacle more comfortably, he crosses his leg over the horse's neck. If enthusiasm seizes him, he climbs slowly down from his horse, uncoils his lasso, and throws it at a bull rushing past him at lightning speed forty paces away. He catches the animal by one foot as he had intended, then quietly recoils his rope.

---

[36] **privations**—lack of basic necessities.

[37] **jaunts**—trips; excursions.

[38] **courser**—horse; charger.

QUESTIONS TO CONSIDER

1. Why do you think the author felt that increased use of Argentina's rivers was so desirable?

2. To what part of the world does the author repeatedly compare Argentina? What does he suggest about Argentina's potential development?

3. What are the positive and negative aspects of the gaucho's way of living as the author sees them?

4. According to Sarmiento, what makes a person civilized?

5. Do you agree that the independence, arrogance, and isolation of the gaucho might have been his greatest advantage? Why or why not?

Mexican Masks

BY OCTAVIO PAZ

Translated by Lysander Kemp, Yara Milos,
and Rachel Phillips Belash

Octavio Paz (Mexico, 1914–1998) was awarded the Nobel Prize
for Literature in 1990. Internationally revered as a poet, editor,
publisher, translator, and art critic, Paz has been credited with
opening the Mexican psyche to Western civilization. His most
famous books are a biography of Sor Juana Inés de la Cruz and
The Labyrinth of Solitude. *The following selection comes from*
a chapter in The Labyrinth of Solitude. *In it, Paz suggests that*
Mexicans hide their true identities behind masks.

> *Impassioned heart, disguise your sorrow . . .*
> —Popular song

The Mexican, whether young or old, criollo[1] or mestizo,[2] general or laborer or lawyer, seems to me to be a person who shuts himself away to protect himself: his face is a mask and so is his smile. In his harsh solitude, which is both **barbed**[3] and courteous, everything serves him as a defense: silence and words, politeness and disdain, irony and resignation. He is jealous of his own privacy and that of others, and he is afraid even to glance at his neighbor, because a mere glance can trigger the rage of these electrically charged spirits. He passes through life like a man who has been **flayed;**[4] everything can hurt him, including words and the very suspicion of words. His language is full of **reticences,**[5] of metaphors and **allusions,**[6] of unfinished phrases, while his silence is full of tints, folds, **thunderheads,**[7] sudden rainbows, indecipherable threats. Even in a quarrel he prefers veiled expressions to outright insults: "A word to the wise is sufficient." He builds a wall of indifference and remoteness between reality and himself, a wall that is no less impenetrable for being invisible. The Mexican is always remote, from the world and from other people. And also from himself.

The speech of our people reflects the extent to which we protect ourselves from the outside world: the ideal of manliness is never to "crack," never to back down. Those who "open themselves up" are cowards. Unlike other people, we believe that opening oneself up is a weakness or a betrayal. The Mexican can bend, can bow humbly, can even stoop, but he cannot back down, that is, he cannot allow the outside world to penetrate

---

[1] criollo—a person of European descent born in Spanish America.

[2] mestizo—a person of mixed racial heritage, especially of mixed European and Native American ancestry.

[3] **barbed**—mean.

[4] **flayed**—stripped of his skin.

[5] **reticences**—reserves; silences.

[6] **allusions**—references to other things.

[7] **thunderheads**—rain clouds.

his privacy. The man who backs down is not to be trusted, is a traitor or a person of doubtful loyalty; he babbles secrets and is incapable of confronting a dangerous situation. Women are inferior beings because, in submitting, they open themselves up. Their inferiority is **constitutional**[8] and resides in their sex, their submissiveness, which is a wound that never heals.

Hermeticism[9] is one of the several recourses of our suspicion and distrust. It shows that we instinctively regard the world around us to be dangerous. This reaction is justifiable if one considers what our history has been and the kind of society we have created. The harshness and hostility of our environment, and the hidden, indefinable threat that is always afloat in the air, oblige us to close ourselves in, like those plants that survive by storing up liquid within their spiny exteriors. But this attitude, legitimate enough in its origins, has become a mechanism that functions automatically. Our response to sympathy and tenderness is reserve, since we cannot tell whether those feelings are genuine or **simulated**.[10] In addition, our masculine integrity is as much endangered by kindness as it is by hostility. Any opening in our defenses is a lessening of our manliness.

Our relationships with other men are always tinged with suspicion. Every time a Mexican confides in a friend or acquaintance, every time he opens himself up, it is an **abdication**.[11] He dreads that the person in whom he has confided will scorn him. Therefore confidences result in dishonor, and they are as dangerous for the person to whom they are made as they are for the person who makes them. We do not drown ourselves, like

---

[8] **constitutional**—inborn; innate.

[9] **Hermeticism**—condition of being sealed off; impenetrable.

[10] **simulated**—false.

[11] **abdication**—giving up.

Narcissus,[12] in the pool that reflects us; we try to stop it up instead. Our anger is prompted not only by the fear of being used by our confidants—that fear is common to everyone—but also by the shame of having renounced our solitude. To confide in others is to dispossess oneself; when we have confided in someone who is not worthy of it, we say, "I sold myself to So-and so." That is, we have "cracked," have let someone into our fortress. The distance between one man and another, which creates mutual respect and mutual security, has disappeared. We are at the mercy of the intruder. What is worse, we have actually abdicated.

All these expressions reveal that the Mexican views life as combat. This attitude does not make him any different from anyone else in the modern world. For other people, however, the manly ideal consists in an open and aggressive fondness for combat, whereas we emphasize defensiveness, the readiness to repel any attack. The Mexican *macho*—the male—is a hermetic being, closed up himself, capable of guarding both himself and whatever has been confided to him. Manliness is judged according to one's invulnerability to enemy arms or the impacts of the outside world. **Stoicism**[13] is the most exalted of our military and political attributes. Our history is full of expressions and incidents that demonstrate the indifference of our heroes toward suffering or danger. We are taught from childhood to accept defeat with dignity, a conception that is certainly not ignoble. And if we are not all good stoics like Juárez and Cuauhtémoc,[14] at least we can be resigned and patient and long-suffering. Resignation is

---

[12] Narcissus—In Greek mythology, he fell in love with his own image in a pool of water.

[13] **Stoicism**—indifference to pleasure or pain.

[14] Juárez . . . Cuauhtémoc—Benito Juárez was president of Mexico in the 1860s. Cuauhtémoc was the last of the Aztec leaders to be tortured by the Spanish conquistadors.

one of our most popular virtues. We admire **fortitude**[15] in the face of adversity more than the most brilliant triumph.

This predominance of the closed over the open manifests itself not only as impassivity and distrust, irony and suspicion, but also as love for Form. Form surrounds and sets bounds to our privacy, limiting its excesses, curbing its explosions, isolating and preserving it. Both our Spanish and Indian heritages have influenced our fondness for ceremony, formulas, and order. A superficial examination of our history might suggest otherwise, but actually the Mexican aspires to create an orderly world regulated by clearly stated principles. The turbulence and **rancor**[16] of our political struggles prove that **juridical**[17] ideas play an important role in our public life. The Mexican also strives to be formal in his daily life, and his formalities are very apt to become formulas. This is not difficult to understand. Order, juridical, social, religious or artistic brings security and stability, and a person has only to adjust to the models and principles that regulate life; he can express himself without resorting to the perpetual inventiveness demanded by a free society. Perhaps our traditionalism, which is one of the constants of our national character, giving coherence to our people and our history, results from our professed love for Form.

No doubt an element of masculine vanity, the vanity of the "señor," of the lord or chieftain (it is an inheritance from both our Indian and Spanish ancestors), enters into our conception of feminine modesty. Like almost all other people, the Mexican considers woman to be an instrument, sometimes of masculine desires, sometimes of the ends assigned to her by morality, society and the law. It must be admitted that she has never been asked

---

[15] **fortitude**—strength of mind.

[16] **rancor**—bitterness; unpleasantness.

[17] **juridical**—legal.

to consent to these ends and that she participates in their realization only passively, as a "repository" for certain values. Whether as prostitute, goddess, *grande dame* or mistress, woman transmits or preserves—but does not believe in—the values and energies entrusted to her by nature or society. In a world made in man's image, woman is only a reflection of masculine will and desire. When passive, she becomes a goddess, a beloved one, a being who embodies the ancient, stable elements of the universe: the earth, motherhood, virginity. When active, she is always function and means, a **receptacle**[18] and a channel. Womanhood, unlike manhood, is never an end in itself.

In other countries these functions are realized in public, often with something of a flair. There are countries that revere prostitutes or virgins, and countries that worship mothers; the *grande dame* is praised and respected almost everywhere. In contrast, we prefer these graces and virtues to be hidden. She should confront the world with an impassive smile. Woman should be secretive. She should be "decent" in the face of erotic excitements and "long suffering" in the face of adversity. In either event her response is neither instinctive nor personal: it conforms to a general model, and it is the defensive and passive aspects of this model, as in the case of the *macho,* that are emphasized, in a gamut ranging from modesty and "decency" to stoicism, resignation and impassivity.

Our Spanish-Arabic inheritance is only a partial explanation of this conduct. The Spanish attitude toward women is very simple. It is expressed quite brutally and concisely in these two sayings: "A woman's place is in the home, with a broken leg" and "Between a female saint and a male saint, a wall of mortared stone." Woman is a domesticated wild animal, lecherous and sinful from birth, who must be subdued with a stick and

---

[18] **receptacle**—container that stores things.

guided by the "reins of religion." Therefore Spaniards consider other women—especially those of a race or religion different from their own—to be easy game. The Mexican considers woman to be a dark, secret and passive being. He does not attribute evil instincts to her; he even pretends that she does not have any. Or, to put it more exactly, her instincts are not her own but those of the species, because she is an **incarnation**[19] of the life force, which is essentially impersonal. Thus it is impossible for her to have a personal, private life, for if she were to be herself—if she were to be mistress of her own wishes, passions or whims—she would be unfaithful to herself. The Mexican, heir to the great pre-Columbian religions based on nature, is a good deal more pagan[20] than the Spaniard, and does not condemn the natural world. Sexual love is not tinged with grief and horror in Mexico as it is in Spain. Instincts themselves are not dangerous; the danger lies in any personal, individual expression of them. And this brings us back to the idea of passivity: woman is never herself, whether lying stretched out or standing up straight, whether naked or fully clothed. She is an undifferentiated manifestation of life, a channel for the universal appetite. In this sense she has no desires of her own.

North Americans also claim that instincts and desires do not exist, but the basis of their pretense is different from ours, even the opposite of it. The North American hides or denies certain parts of his body and, more often, of his psyche: they are immoral, ergo they do not exist. By denying them he inhibits his spontaneity. The Mexican woman quite simply has no will of her own. Her body is asleep and only comes really alive when someone awakens her. She is an answer rather than a question, a vibrant and easily worked material

---

[19] **incarnation**—embodiment in human form.

[20] pagan—non-Christian.

that is shaped by the imagination and sensuality of the male. In other countries women are active, attempting to attract men through the agility of their minds or the seductivity of their bodies, but the Mexican woman has a sort of **hieratic**[21] calm, a tranquillity made up of both hope and contempt. The man circles around her, courts her, sings to her, sets his horse (or his imagination) to performing *caracoles*[22] for her pleasure. Meanwhile she remains behind the veil of her modesty and immobility. She is an idol, and like all idols she is mistress of magnetic forces whose **efficacy**[23] increases as their source of transmission becomes more and more passive and secretive. There is a cosmic analogy here: woman does not seek, she attracts, and the center of attraction is her hidden, passive sexuality. It is a secret and immobile sun.

The falsity of this conception is obvious enough when one considers the Mexican woman's sensitivity and restlessness, but at least it does not turn her into an object, a mere thing. She is a symbol, like all women, of the stability and continuity of the race. In addition to her cosmic significance she has an important social role, which is to see to it that law and order, piety and tenderness are predominant in everyday life. We will not allow anyone to be disrespectful to women, and although this is doubtless a universal notion, the Mexican carries it to its ultimate consequences. Thanks to woman, many of the **asperities**[24] of "man-to-man" relationships are softened. Of course we should ask the Mexican woman for her own opinion, because this "respect" is often a hypocritical way of subjecting her and preventing her from expressing herself. Perhaps she would usually prefer to be treated with less "respect"

[21] **hieratic**—symbolic; resembling an idol or deity.

[22] *caracoles*—dances.

[23] **efficacy**—effectiveness.

[24] **asperities**—sharpnesses; bitternesses.

(which anyway is granted to her only in public) and with greater freedom and truthfulness; that is, to be treated as a human being rather than as a symbol or function. But how can we agree to let her express herself when our whole way of life is a mask designed to hide our intimate feelings?

Despite her modesty and the **vigilance**[25] of society, woman is always vulnerable. Her social situation—as the **repository**[26] of honor, in the Spanish sense—and the misfortune of her "open" anatomy expose her to all kinds of dangers, against which neither personal morality nor masculine protection is sufficient. She is submissive and open by nature. But, through a compensation-mechanism that is easily explained, her natural frailty is made a virtue and the myth of the "long-suffering Mexican woman" is created. The idol—always vulnerable, always in process of transforming itself into a human being—becomes a victim, but a victim hardened and insensible to suffering, bearing her **tribulations**[27] in silence. (A "long-suffering" person is less sensitive to pain than a person whom adversity has hardly touched.) Through suffering our women become like our men: invulnerable, able, impassive, and stoic.

It might be said that by turning what ought to be a cause for shame into a virtue, we are only trying to relieve our guilt feelings and cover up a cruel reality. This is true, but it is also true that in attributing to her the same invulnerability that we strive to achieve ourselves, we provide her with a moral immunity to shield her unfortunate anatomical openness. Thanks to suffering and her ability to endure it without protest, she transcends her condition and acquires the same attributes as men.

---

[25] **vigilance**—watchfulness.

[26] **repository**—trusted person.

[27] **tribulations**—problems; suffering.

It is interesting to note that the image of the *mala mujer*—the "bad woman"—is almost always accompanied by the idea of aggressive activity. She is not passive like the "self-denying mother," the "waiting sweetheart," the hermetic idol: she comes and goes, she looks for men and then leaves them. Her extreme mobility, through a mechanism similar to that described above, renders her invulnerable. Activity and immodesty unite to **petrify**[28] her soul. The *mala* is hard and impious and independent like the *macho*. In her own way she also transcends her physiological weakness and closes herself off from the world.

It is likewise significant that masculine homosexuality is regarded with a certain indulgence insofar as the active agent is concerned. The passive agent is an abject, degraded being. This ambiguous conception is made very clear in the word games or battles—full of obscene allusions and double meanings—that are so popular in Mexico City. Each of the speakers tries to humiliate his adversary with verbal traps and ingenious linguistic combinations, and the loser is the person who cannot think of a comeback, who has to swallow his opponent's jibes.

These jibes are full of aggressive sexual allusions; the loser is possessed, is violated, by the winner, and the spectators laugh and sneer at him. Masculine homosexuality is tolerated, then, on condition that it consists in violating a passive agent. As with heterosexual relationships, the important thing is not to open oneself up and at the same time to break open one's opponent.

* * *

It seems to me that all of these attitudes, however different their sources, testify to actions to the "closed" nature of our reactions to the world around us or to

---

[28] **petrify**—harden.

our fellows. But our mechanisms of defense and self-preservation are not enough, and therefore we make use of **dissimulation**,[29] which is almost habitual with us. It does not increase our passivity; on the contrary, it demands an active inventiveness and must reshape itself from one moment to another. We tell lies for the mere pleasure of it, like all imaginative peoples, but we also tell lies to hide ourselves and protect ourselves from intruders. Lying plays a decisive role in our daily lives, our politics, our love-affairs and our friendships, and since we attempt to deceive ourselves as well as others, our lies are brilliant and fertile, not like the gross inventions of other peoples. Lying is a tragic game in which we risk a part of our very selves. Hence it is pointless to denounce it.

The **dissembler**[30] pretends to be someone he is not. His role requires constant improvisation, a steady forward progress across shifting sands. Every moment he must remake, re-create, modify the personage he is playing, until at last the moment arrives when reality and appearance, the lie and the truth, are one. At first the pretense is only a fabric of inventions intended to baffle our neighbors, but eventually it becomes a superior—because more artistic—form of reality. Our lies reflect both what we lack and what we desire, both what we are not and what we would like to be. . . .

If we can arrive at authenticity by means of lies, an excess of sincerity can bring us to refined forms of lying. When we fall in love we open ourselves up and reveal our intimate feelings, because an ancient tradition requires that the man suffering from love display his wounds to the loved one. But in displaying them the lover transforms himself into an image, an object he presents for the loved one's—and his own—contemplation. He asks her to regard him with the same

---

[29] **dissimulation**—pretense; imposture.

[30] **dissembler**—one who pretends; liar.

worshipful eyes with which he regards himself. And now the looks of others do not strip him naked; instead, they clothe him in piety. He has offered himself as a spectacle, asking the spectators to see him as he sees himself, and in so doing he has escaped from the game of love, has saved his true self by replacing it with an image.

Human relationships run the risk, in all lands and ages, of becoming **equivocal**.[31] This is especially true of love. Narcissism and **masochism**[32] are not exclusively Mexican traits, but it is notable how often our popular songs and sayings and our everyday behavior treat love as falsehood and betrayal. We almost always evade the perils of a naked relationship by exaggerating our feelings. At the same time, the combative nature of our eroticism is emphasized and aggravated. Love is an attempt to penetrate another being, but it can only be realized if the surrender is mutual. It is always difficult to give oneself up; few persons anywhere ever succeed in doing so, and even fewer transcend the possessive stage to know love for what it actually is: a perpetual discovery, an immersion in the waters of reality, and an unending recreation. The Mexican conceives of love as combat and conquest. It is not so much an attempt to penetrate reality by means of the body as it is to violate it. Therefore the image of the fortunate lover derived, perhaps, from the Spanish Don Juan—is confused with that of the man who deliberately makes use of his feelings, real or invented, to win possession of a woman.

Dissimulation is an activity very much like that of actors in the theater, but the true actor surrenders himself to the role he is playing and embodies it fully, even though he sloughs[33] it off again, like a snake its skin, when the final curtain comes down. The dissembler

---

[31] **equivocal**—of a doubtful or uncertain nature.

[32] **masochism**—the enjoyment of being abused or mistreated.

[33] sloughs—sheds.

never surrenders or forgets himself, because he would no longer be dissembling if he became one with his image. But this fiction becomes an inseparable—and **spurious**[34]—part of his nature. He is condemned to play his role throughout life, since the pact between himself and his impersonation cannot be broken except by death or sacrifice. The lie takes command of him and becomes the very foundation of his personality.

---

[34] **spurious**—false.

QUESTIONS TO CONSIDER

1. Why does Paz believe the Mexican shuts himself away to protect himself?

2. Why does he believe that to confide in someone is an abdication?

3. Paz writes, "the Mexican views life as combat." How does he feel about that? How do you feel?

Ode to the Onion

BY PABLO NERUDA

Translated by María Jacketti

One of the most beloved of Latin American poets, Pablo Neruda (Chile, 1904–1973) earned the Nobel Prize for Literature in 1971. Among his most celebrated works are Residence on Earth, España in Our Hearts, *and* Canto General. *A devoted communist, Neruda wrote poetry that reflected his interest in politics and concern for the less fortunate. In the following poem, Neruda praises the onion for its unique beauty and tremendous value to the poor.*

Onion,
luminous globe,
petal by petal,
your splendor appeared;
crystal scales multiplied within your essence,
and beneath the secret of the rich earth,
your dewy belly grew round. The miracle
was born underground,

and when your heavy green stem appeared,
and your leaves were born
like swords in the vegetable patch,
the earth accumulated riches,
exposing your naked transparency,
and as with Aphrodite,[1] the remote sea
imitated the magnolia
by lifting its breasts;
likewise, the earth
created you,
onion,
clear as a planet,
and destined
to shine,
a steadfast constellation,
round sea rose
on
poverty's table.

Endowed[2] with abundance,
you break
your fresh globe
in sizzling marriage
with the stew pot;
when you touch hot oil,
crystal slivers become
curled feathers of gold.

I will also remember your abundant
and loving influence on salads;
it seems the sky also contributed
giving you the fine form of hail

---

[1] Aphrodite—in Greek mythology, the goddess of beauty who rose out of sea foam.

[2] **Endowed**—supplied.

in celebration of your **diced**[3] clarity
when sprinkled over the tomato's planetary halves.
But when you reach
the hands of the people,
dappled with oil,
and dusted
with a little salt,
you silence a worker's hunger
along difficult roads.
Star of the poor,
fairy godmother
sheathed[4]
in airy
paper,
you exit the earth,
eternal, untouched, pure:
a star-seed.
And when the kitchen knife
slices you,
a painless tear is
shed.
You made us cry without **affliction.**[5]
Throughout my days,
I've celebrated the onion.
In my eyes
you are more lovely
than a bird with blinding feathers.
In my eyes
you are a **celestial**[6] globe, a platinum cup,

---

[3] **diced**—sliced into cubes.

[4] **sheathed**—covered.

[5] **affliction**—cause of pain or suffering.

[6] **celestial**—heavenly.

the **quiescent**[7] dance
of an anemone[8] in the snow.
And the fragrance of the land lives
within your crystalline nature.

---

[7] **quiescent**—quiet.

[8] anemone—brightly colored flower.

QUESTIONS TO CONSIDER

1. Why do you think Neruda refers to the onion as the "Star of the poor"?

2. How does Neruda's praise of the onion change or reinforce your opinion about the simple things in life?

Poems of the Home

BY GABRIELA MISTRAL

Translated by Alice Stone Blackwell

Gabriela Mistral (Chile, 1889–1957) was born Lucila Godoy Alcayagaó. She won the Nobel Prize for Literature in 1945, becoming the first Latin American woman to earn such an honor. Mistral enjoyed great success throughout her career, gaining particular praise for her novels, Ternura *and* Tala. *In the poems that follow, Mistral shows how such ordinary items as a lamp, brazier, and jar enliven a home.*

The Lamp

Blessed be my lamp! It does not overwhelm me like the blaze of the sun, and it has a softened glance: of pure gentleness, of pure sweetness.

    It burns in the middle of my room; it is its soul. Its **subdued**[1] reflection hardly makes my tears glitter, and I do not see them as they run over my breast.

---

[1] **subdued**—less intense; weak.

According to the dream that is in my heart, I change its little crystal head. For my prayer, I give it a blue light, and my room becomes like the depths of the valley— now that I no longer raise my prayer from the bottom of the valleys. For my sadness, it has a violet crystal, and makes things suffer with me. It knows more of my life than the breasts on which I have **reposed.**[2] It is alive, because it has touched my heart so many nights. It has the soft warmth of my inner wound, which now does not burn—which, because it has lasted so long, has become very soft.

Perhaps, at nightfall, the dead, who have no power of sight, come to seek it in the eyes of the lamps. Who can that dead man be, who is gazing at me with so much silent gentleness?

If it were human, it would grow weary in the presence of my suffering, or else, full of solicitude, it would wish to be with me still when the mercy of sleep comes. Then it is perfection.

It cannot be perceived from without, and my enemies who pass believe that I am alone. To all my possessions, as small as it, as divine as it, I give an **imperceptible**[3] brightness to defend them from the thieves of happiness.

Enough for me is what its halo of light **illumines.**[4] It has room for my mother's face and the open book. Let them leave me only what this lamp bathes in its light; they may **dispossess**[5] me of all beside!

I ask of God that tonight no sad soul may lack a soft lamp to dim the brightness of its tears!

---

[2] **reposed**—rested.

[3] **imperceptible**—not perceivable with the senses; intangible.

[4] **illumines**—brightens.

[5] **dispossess**—seize; take from.

The Brazier

Brazier[6] of jewels, illusion for the poor! When we look at you, we possess precious stones.

All through the night I keep on enjoying the degrees of your warmth. First it is the live coal, naked as a wound; afterwards a thin covering of ashes that gives you the tint of the paler roses; and at the night's end, a light, soft whiteness that wraps you in a shroud.

While you burn, dreams and memories keep enkindling, and then, with the slowness of your embers, they go on to veil themselves and die.

You are intimacy; without you there is the house, but we do not feel it to be the home.

You teach me that what burns gathers beings around its flame; and as I gazed at you, when a little girl, I thought to turn back my heart thus; and I imagined the dance of the children going on around me.

The hands of my own people are joined over your live coals. Although life has scattered us, we have to remember that interlacing of the hands, woven around you.

To enjoy you better, I leave you uncovered; I do not let them cover your wonderful embers.

They have given you an **aureole**[7] of bronze, and it ennobles you, widening your splendor.

My grandmothers burned mint in you to put the evil spirits to flight, and I too, in order to remind you of them am wont[8] to scatter over you fragrant herbs, which crackle upon your embers like kisses.

When I gaze at you, ancient brazier of my home, I say: May all the poor light you tonight, to put their sad hands together over you with love!

---

[6] Brazier—metal pan holding burning coals.

[7] **aureole**—halo.

[8] wont—likely.

The Earthen Jar

Earthen jar, dark as my cheek, how easy of access you are to my thirst!

Better than you is the lip of the spring, open in the ravine; but it is far away, and on this summer night I cannot go to it.

I fill you, slowly, every morning. At first the water sings as it falls; when it remains silent, I kiss it on its **tremulous**[9] mouth, paying it for its gift.

You are graceful and strong, dark jar. You are like the bosom of a countrywoman who nursed me when my mother's breast failed. I remember her when I look at you, and I feel of your outlines with tenderness.

Do you see my dry lips? They are lips that hold many thirsts for God, for beauty, for love. None of these has been like you, simple and obedient; and the three continue to make my lips white.

As I love you, I never set a cup beside you; I drink from your lip itself, holding you in the curve of my arm. If in your silence you are dreaming of an embrace, I give you the illusion that you have it.

Do you feel my tenderness?

In summer I put under you fine sand, golden and damp, to keep the heat away from you; and once I covered a little break in you softly with fresh clay. I have been slow for many labors, but I have always loved to be the sweet mistress, who takes hold of things with a trembling gentleness, if perchance they understand, if perchance they suffer, like her.

Tomorrow, when I go to the field, I shall gather sprays of mint to bring to you and submerge in your water. You will smell the field in the odor of my hands.

---

[9] **tremulous**—trembling; shaking.

QUESTIONS TO CONSIDER

1. The speaker describes her lamp as the soul of her room. How does she establish this idea?

2. Why do you think the poet says that without the brazier a house is not a home?

3. Why does the poet associate the earthen jar with herself and with her people?

4. What everyday items from your home seem to you to represent your life there? How might you explore this idea in a poem?

Balthazar's Marvelous Afternoon

BY GABRIEL GARCÍA MÁRQUEZ

Translated by Gerome Bernstein

*Awarded the Nobel Prize for Literature in 1982, Gabriel García
Márquez (Colombia, 1928–) is credited with leading an innovative
generation of writers immersed in the "magical realist" style.
His most famous works are* One Hundred Years of Solitude,
Chronicle of a Death Foretold, *and* Love in the Time of
Cholera. *Although perhaps best known for his novels, García
Márquez also writes short stories with exemplary skill. In
"Balthazar's Marvelous Afternoon," he portrays a man's struggle
to maintain dignity in an increasingly material society.*

The cage was finished. Balthazar hung it under the eave,[1] from force of habit, and when he finished lunch everyone was already saying that it was the most beautiful cage in the world. So many people came to see it that a crowd formed in front of the house, and Balthazar had to take it down and close the shop.

"You have to shave," Ursula, his wife, told him. "You look like a *Capuchin*."[2]

"It's bad to shave after lunch," said Balthazar.

He had two weeks' growth, short, hard, and bristly hair like the mane of a mule, and the general expression of a frightened boy. But it was a false expression. In February he was thirty; he had been living with Ursula for four years, without marrying her and without having children, and life had given him many reasons to be on guard but none to be frightened. He did not even know that for some people the cage he had just made was the most beautiful one in the world. For him, accustomed to making cages since childhood, it had been hardly any more difficult than the others.

"Then rest for a while," said the woman. "With that beard you can't show yourself anywhere."

While he was resting, he had to get out of his hammock several times to show the cage to the neighbors. Ursula had paid little attention to it until then. She was annoyed because her husband had neglected the work of his carpenter's shop to devote himself entirely to the cage, and for two weeks had slept poorly, turning over and muttering **incoherencies**,[3] and he hadn't thought of shaving. But her annoyance dissolved in the face of the finished cage. When Balthazar woke up from his nap, she had ironed his

---

[1] eave—projecting overhang at the lower edge of a roof.

[2] *Capuchin*—monk.

[3] **incoherencies**—unclear, not understandable, speeches.

pants and a shirt; she had put them on a chair near the hammock and had carried the cage to the dining table. She regarded it in silence.

"How much will you charge?" she asked.

"I don't know," Balthazar answered. "I'm going to ask for thirty pesos to see if they'll give me twenty."

"Ask for fifty," said Ursula. "You've lost a lot of sleep in these two weeks. Furthermore, it's rather large. I think it's the biggest cage I've ever seen in my life."

Balthazar began to shave.

"Do you think they'll give me fifty pesos?"

"That's nothing for Mr. Chepe Montiel, and the cage is worth it," said Ursula. "You should ask for sixty."

The house lay in the stifling shadow. It was the first week of April and the heat seemed less bearable because of the chirping of the cicadas.[4] When he finished dressing, Balthazar opened the door to the patio to cool off the house, and a group of children entered the dining room.

The news had spread. Dr. Octavio Giraldo, an old physician, happy with life but tired of his profession, thought about Balthazar's cage while he was eating lunch with his **invalid**[5] wife. On the inside terrace, where they put the table on hot days, there were many flowerpots and two cages with canaries. His wife liked birds, and she liked them so much that she hated cats because they could eat them up. Thinking about her, Dr. Giraldo went to see a patient that afternoon, and when he returned he went by Balthazar's house to inspect the cage.

There were a lot of people in the dining room. The cage was on display on the table: with its enormous dome of wire, three stories inside, with passageways and compartments especially for eating and sleeping and

---

[4] cicadas—grasshopper-like insects that make high-pitched sounds.

[5] **invalid**—disabled.

swings in the space set aside for the birds' recreation, it seemed like a small-scale model of a gigantic ice factory. The doctor inspected it carefully, without touching it, thinking that in effect the cage was better than its reputation, and much more beautiful than any he had ever dreamed of for his wife.

"This is a flight of the imagination," he said. He sought out Balthazar among the group of people and, fixing his **maternal**[6] eyes on him, added, "You would have been an extraordinary architect."

Balthazar blushed.

"Thank you," he said.

"It's true," said the doctor. He was smoothly and delicately fat, like a woman who had been beautiful in her youth, and he had delicate hands. His voice seemed like that of a priest speaking Latin. "You wouldn't even need to put birds in it," he said, making the cage turn in front of the audience's eyes as if he were auctioning it off. "It would be enough to hang it in the trees so it could sing by itself." He put it back on the table, thought a moment, looking at the cage, and said:

"Fine, then I'll take it."

"It's sold," said Ursula.

"It belongs to the son of Mr. Chepe Montiel," said Balthazar. "He ordered it specially."

The doctor adopted a respectful attitude.

"Did he give you the design?"

"No," said Balthazar. "He said he wanted a large cage, like this one, for a pair of troupials."[7]

The doctor looked at the cage.

"But this isn't for troupials."

"Of course it is, Doctor," said Balthazar, approaching the table. The children surrounded him. "The measurements are carefully calculated," he said, pointing to the

---

[6] **maternal**—motherly.

[7] troupials—tropical American birds.

different compartments with his forefinger. Then he struck the dome with his knuckles, and the cage filled with **resonant**[8] chords.

"It's the strongest wire you can find, and each joint is **soldered**[9] outside and in," he said.

"It's even big enough for a parrot," interrupted one of the children.

"That it is," said Balthazar.

The doctor turned his head.

"Fine, but he didn't give you the design," he said. "He gave you no exact specifications, aside from making it a cage big enough for troupials. Isn't that right?"

"That's right," said Balthazar.

"Then there's no problem," said the doctor. "One thing is a cage big enough for troupials, and another is this cage. There's no proof that this one is the one you were asked to make."

"It's this very one," said Balthazar, confused. "That's why I made it."

The doctor made an impatient gesture.

"You could make another one," said Ursula, looking at her husband. And then, to the doctor: "You're not in any hurry."

"I promised it to my wife for this afternoon," said the doctor.

"I'm very sorry, Doctor," said Balthazar, "but I can't sell you something that's sold already."

The doctor shrugged his shoulders. Drying the sweat from his neck with a handkerchief, he contemplated the cage silently with the fixed, unfocused gaze of one who looks at a ship which is sailing away.

"How much did they pay you for it?"

Balthazar sought out Ursula's eyes without replying.

"Sixty pesos," she said.

---

[8] **resonant**—resounding; deep in tone.

[9] **soldered**—welded.

The doctor kept looking at the cage. "It's very pretty." He sighed.

"Extremely pretty." Then, moving toward the door, he began to fan himself energetically, smiling, and the trace of that episode disappeared forever from his memory.

"Montiel is very rich," he said.

In truth, José Montiel was not as rich as he seemed, but he would have been capable of doing anything to become so. A few blocks from there, in a house crammed with equipment, where no one had ever smelled a smell that couldn't be sold, he remained indifferent to the news of the cage. His wife, tortured by an obsession with death, closed the doors and windows after lunch and lay for two hours with her eyes opened to the shadow of the room, while José Montiel took his siesta. The clamor of many voices surprised her there. Then she opened the door to the living room and found a crowd in front of the house, and Balthazar with the cage in the middle of the crowd, dressed in white, freshly shaved, with that expression of **decorous**[10] **candor**[11] with which the poor approach the houses of the wealthy.

"What a marvelous thing!" José Montiel's wife exclaimed, with a **radiant**[12] expression, leading Balthazar inside. "I've never seen anything like it in my life," she said, and added, annoyed by the crowd which piled up at the door:

"But bring it inside before they turn the living room into a **grandstand**."[13]

Balthazar was no stranger to José Montiel's house. On different occasions, because of his skill and **forthright**[14] way of dealing, he had been called in to do

---

[10] **decorous**—proper.

[11] **candor**—frankness; sincerity.

[12] **radiant**—bright; beaming.

[13] **grandstand**—roofed stand for spectators at a stadium or racetrack.

[14] **forthright**—straightforward; direct.

minor carpentry jobs. But he never felt at ease among the rich. He used to think about them, about their ugly and argumentative wives, about their tremendous surgical operations, and he always experienced a feeling of pity. When he entered their houses, he couldn't move without dragging his feet.

"Is Pepe home?" he asked.

He had put the cage on the dining-room table.

"He's at school," said José Montiel's wife. "But he shouldn't be long," and she added, "Montiel is taking a bath."

In reality, José Montiel had not had time to bathe. He was giving himself an urgent alcohol rub, in order to come out and see what was going on. He was such a cautious man that he slept without an electric fan so he could watch over the noises of the house while he slept.

"Adelaide!" he shouted. "What's going on?"

"Come and see what a marvelous thing!" his wife shouted.

José Montiel, obese and hairy, his towel draped around his neck, appeared at the bedroom window.

"What is that?"

"Pepe's cage," said Balthazar.

His wife looked at him **perplexedly.**[15]

"Whose?"

"Pepe's," replied Balthazar. And then, turning toward José Montiel, "Pepe ordered it."

Nothing happened at that instant, but Balthazar felt as if someone had just opened the bathroom door on him. José Montiel came out of the bedroom in his underwear.

"Pepe!" he shouted.

"He's not back," whispered his wife, motionless.

Pepe appeared in the doorway. He was about twelve, and had the same curved eyelashes and was as quietly pathetic as his mother.

---

[15] **perplexedly**—in a confused or puzzled manner.

"Come here," José Montiel said to him. "Did you order this?"

The child lowered his head. Grabbing him by the hair, José Montiel forced Pepe to look him in the eye.

"Answer me."

The child bit his lip without replying.

"Montiel," whispered his wife.

José Montiel let the child go and turned toward Balthazar in a fury. "I'm very sorry, Balthazar," he said. "But you should have consulted me before going on. Only to you would it occur to contract[16] with a minor." As he spoke, his face recovered its **serenity**.[17] He lifted the cage without looking at it and gave it to Balthazar.

"Take it away at once, and try to sell it to whomever you can," he said. "Above all, I beg you not to argue with me." He patted him on the back and explained, "The doctor has forbidden me to get angry."

The child had remained motionless, without blinking, until Balthazar looked at him uncertainly with the cage in his hand. Then he emitted a **guttural**[18] sound, like a dog's growl, and threw himself on the floor screaming.

José Montiel looked at him, unmoved, while the mother tried to **pacify**[19] him. "Don't even pick him up," he said. "Let him break his head on the floor, and then put salt and lemon on it so he can rage to his heart's content." The child was shrieking tearlessly while his mother held him by the wrists.

"Leave him alone," José Montiel insisted.

Balthazar observed the child as he would have observed the death **throes**[20] of a **rabid**[21] animal. It was

---

[16] contract—make an agreement.

[17] **serenity**—calm; tranquility.

[18] **guttural**—harsh; throaty.

[19] **pacify**—calm; ease.

[20] **throes**—struggle.

[21] **rabid**—rabies-infested.

almost four o'clock. At that hour, at his house, Ursula was singing a very old song and cutting slices of onion.

"Pepe," said Balthazar.

He approached the child, smiling, and held the cage out to him. The child jumped up, embraced the cage which was almost as big as he was, and stood looking at Balthazar through the wirework without knowing what to say. He hadn't shed one tear.

"Balthazar," said José Montiel softly. "I told you already to take it away."

"Give it back," the woman ordered the child.

"Keep it," said Balthazar. And then, to José Montiel: "After all, that's what I made it for."

José Montiel followed him into the living room.

"Don't be foolish, Balthazar," he was saying, blocking his path. "Take your piece of furniture home and don't be silly. I have no intention of paying you a cent."

"It doesn't matter," said Balthazar. "I made it expressly as a gift for Pepe. I didn't expect to charge anything for it."

As Balthazar made his way through the spectators who were blocking the door, José Montiel was shouting in the middle of the living room. He was very pale and his eyes were beginning to get red.

"Idiot!" he was shouting. "Take your trinket out of here. The last thing we need is for some nobody to give orders in my house. . . ."

In the pool hall, Balthazar was received with an ovation. Until that moment, he thought that he had made a better cage than ever before, that he'd had to give it to the son of José Montiel so he wouldn't keep crying, and that none of these things was particularly important. But then he realized that all of this had a certain importance for many people, and he felt a little excited.

"So they gave you fifty pesos for the cage."

"Sixty," said Balthazar.

"Score one for you, " someone said. "You're the only one who has managed to get such a pile of money out of Mr. Chepe Montiel. We have to celebrate."

They bought him a beer, and Balthazar responded with a round for everybody. Since it was the first time he had ever been out drinking, by dusk he was completely drunk, and he was talking about a fabulous project of a thousand cages, at sixty pesos each, and then of a million cages, till he had sixty million pesos. "We have to make a lot of things to sell to the rich before they die," he was saying, blind drunk. "All of them are sick, and they're going to die. They're so screwed up they can't even get angry any more." For two hours he was paying for the jukebox, which played without interruption. Everybody toasted Balthazar's health, good luck, and fortune, and the death of the rich, but at mealtime they left him alone in the pool hall.

Ursula had waited for him until eight, with a dish of fried meat covered with slices of onion. Someone told her that her husband was in the pool hall, **delirious**[22] with happiness, buying beers for everyone, but she didn't believe it, because Balthazar had never got drunk. When she went to bed, almost at midnight, Balthazar was in a lighted room where there were little tables, each with four chairs, and an outdoor dance floor, where the plovers[23] were walking around. His face was smeared with rouge, and since he couldn't take one more step, he thought he wanted to lie down with two women in the same bed. He had spent so much that he had had to leave his watch in **pawn**,[24] with the promise to pay the next day. A moment later, spread-eagled in the street, he

---

[22] **delirious**—ecstatic; excited.

[23] plovers—wading birds with round bodies and short bills.

[24] **pawn**—security for a loan.

realized that his shoes were being taken off, but he didn't want to abandon the happiest dream of his life. The women who passed on their way to five-o'clock Mass didn't dare look at him, thinking he was dead.

QUESTIONS TO CONSIDER

1. How are Balthazar and Ursula different?

2. How does García Márquez depict relations between people in the upper and lower classes? Support your answers with examples from the text.

3. What role does García Márquez assign to the artist in this society?

4. Why do you think Balthazar reacts so recklessly at the end of the story?

The Return

BY ROSARIO CASTELLANOS

Translated by Magda Bogin

Raised in an aristocratic family, Rosario Castellanos (Mexico, 1925–1974) broke away from her upper-class background to chronicle the lives of minority groups in Mexico. She has given voice to many women and Indians by placing them at the forefront of her literature. Castellanos has written such acclaimed novels as Balun Canan, City of Kings, *and* Meditation on the Threshold. *She also has been lauded for her essays, in which she often weaves intellectual observations with personal anecdotes. In "The Return," Castellanos shows how images of the past continue to haunt the present and shape people's lives.*

I walk the land of Anahuac which is the land of my dead.

Yes: as their names suggest—and other signs—they are dead. They do not speak.

Some, the most recent, have their chins tied with
the final kerchief. Others with their jaw intact, calcium
reverted to its mute mineral state.

So, then, do not ask me to live for them. To see the
world they do not see, to body forth a destiny left
incomplete.

If I need justification for existing, for doing and, above
all, for not erasing myself (which would be logical
based on the evidence) I will have to obtain it some
other way.

From the living, who turn their backs on me, who do
not see me but who if they did would reject me like
those who know that, by a law of nature, fewer bodies
mean more space and air and hope?

From those who arrive with the grenade already
poised[1] to explode between their hands? From those
who see in me an obstacle, a ruin, a hideous sight
that must be destroyed in order to construct the new?

No. The answer will not come from humans alone.

Perhaps to undertake some great work . . . Work?
Change nature's face? Add some book to the
bibliographies? Change the course of history?

But that's a man's job—again—cut to time measured
to fit men following the criteria they use to accept or
reject.

Then what? God? His reign? It is too late now to
invent or return to golden childhood.

---

[1] **poised**—positioned.

Just accept the facts: you are here and it's all the same as if you had stayed or never left. The same. For you. For everyone.

Superfluous[2] here. Superfluous there. Superfluous exactly like each and every one you see and do not see.

No one is necessary not even for you, who by definition are so needy.

---

[2] **Superfluous**—beyond what is required or sufficient.

QUESTIONS TO CONSIDER

1. For whom does the poem seem to speak?

2. To what natural law does the speaker refer in the sixth stanza? How does the speaker think this law might affect others' treatment of her?

3. What justification for living do you think the speaker might find among living people?

Historical Overview

The Colonial Era (1492–1830) *When the Europeans reached present-day Latin America in the late 1400s, the native Aztec, Mayan, and Incan civilizations were thriving. But as more Europeans arrived, more and more Indians died, victims of disease and war. The Spanish and Portuguese quickly conquered the Indian empires and took over the Americas. It would be more than three hundred years before Latin American countries gained their freedom.*

Background The Pyramids of the Sun and Moon in Teotihuacan, Mexico, a legacy of pre-Columbian civilization.

Spanish-style city squares, like the Plaza de Bolívar in Colombia, abound in Latin America. They are everlasting proof of European influence.

European colonizers stake their claim in the Americas, from a mural by Diego Rivera.

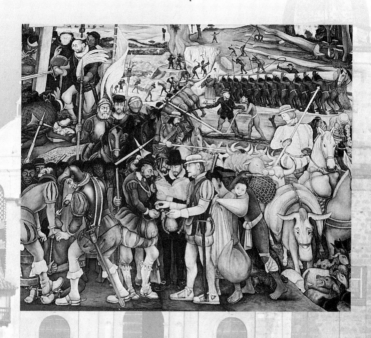

Independence (1810–1830) *Indians, black slaves, and disgruntled aristocrats throughout Latin America had long been dissatisfied with colonial rule. But achieving independence proved immensely difficult. Latin American freedom fighters were not well equipped nor skilled to battle the colonialists. Ever disorganized, they could not even agree upon what to do after they had won. While independence meant an end to colonial rule, it marked the beginning of a whole new era of struggle.*

Background A monument celebrates Rondon's Lancers, who defeated Spanish soldiers in a hard-fought battle.

A statue of Simón Bolívar, Bolivia's famous independence warrior and statesman, stands in a plaza in Colombia. ▶

▲
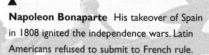
Napoleon Bonaparte His takeover of Spain
in 1808 ignited the independence wars. Latin
Americans refused to submit to French rule.

▲

A Colombian man cuts sugar cane in preparation for its export.

Post-Independence (1830–1930) *The wars of independence proved devastating to the Latin American economies. New governments had to cope with heavy debts, an empty treasury, and an impoverished public. They relied first on Britain, and later on the United States, for loans and investments. But this arrangement only pushed Latin America further into debt. With the economy in shambles, social relations and confidence in national leaders were unraveling.*

Background In Peru, Indian llamas carry barley, a crucial part of the export economy.

President Theodore Roosevelt applied his Big Stick policy in the Americas, drawing many countries under his control by warning the European powers to stay out of the Western hemisphere.

The Panama Canal was completed in 1914. It created a quick water route between New York and California and increased the United States' influence in much of Latin American politics.

▼

Dictatorship and Authoritarianism (1930–1989)

In addition to struggling to control the economy, Latin American political leaders struggled to control their citizens. Poor and frustrated, the people demanded change and a better way of life. In an effort to maintain order, the militaries of many nations overthrew the government leaders and terrorized the people into obedience. As dictators, they ruled absolutely and undemocratically. The move toward democracy followed the economic upturn of the late 1980s—far too late for the thousands who had already suffered under the brutal regimes.

▲
The Mothers of the Missing March, June 10, 1982. Mothers of missing Argentine men and women marched in Buenos Aires, blaming the government for the disappearance of more than 30,000 people since 1976.

◀ **General Augusto Pinochet** He seized power in Chile in 1973 and began 17 years of heavy-handed rule. Here he stands under close guard at a rally.

Background Argentinean leader Juan Perón and his wife Eva wave to the crowd during the presidential inauguration of 1952. Perón was overthrown in 1955.

Political Evolution (1990s) *While tyranny no longer reigns supreme in Latin America, democracy is still fragile. Governments depend on the United States and other countries for loans, masses of people live in poverty, and race relations are extremely tense. But Latin America has proven its determination over the centuries and will continue to fight for stability and prosperity.*

Pope John Paul II and Fidel Castro stand side by side at a welcoming ceremony in Cuba in 1998. The Pope's historic visit to the island demonstrated Castro's increased participation in world affairs. ▶

Mexican President Ernesto Zedillo greets his supporters. Sitting presidents used to choose their successors, but a new national law passed in May, 1999, allows voters to choose the presidential nominees in primary elections.
▼

▲
A Guatemalan mother and baby in traditional Indian dress. Indians now enjoy more rights than ever before, though they still struggle to maintain their ethnic identities and customs.

chapter three

Through a
Glass Darkly

The Feather Pillow

BY HORACIO QUIROGA

Translated by Margaret Sayers Peden

Often described as the Edgar Allan Poe of Latin America, Horacio Quiroga (Uruguay, 1878–1937) wrote haunting works about death. His dark literature reflects his equally gloomy life, which was marred by the deaths of his father, stepfather, and wife. Quiroga took his own life after discovering he was ill with cancer. Despite these tragic events, Quiroga was a highly successful writer. In "The Feather Pillow," he tells a horrific tale about misguided love.

Her entire honeymoon gave her hot and cold shivers. A blond, angelic, and timid young girl, the childish fancies she had dreamed about being a bride had been chilled by her husband's rough character. She loved him very much, nonetheless, although sometimes she gave a light shudder when, as they returned home through the streets together at night, she cast a **furtive**[1] glance at the

---

[1] **furtive**—sly; shifty.

impressive stature of her Jordan, who had been silent for an hour. He, for his part, loved her profoundly but never let it be seen.

For three months—they had been married in April—they lived in a special kind of bliss. Doubtless she would have wished less severity in the rigorous sky of love, more expansive and less cautious tenderness, but her husband's impassive manner always restrained her.

The house in which they lived influenced her chills and shuddering to no small degree. The whiteness of the silent patio—friezes,[2] columns, and marble statues—produced the wintry impression of an enchanted palace. Inside, the glacial brilliance of stucco, the completely bare walls, affirmed the sensation of unpleasant coldness. As one crossed from one room to another, the echo of his steps reverberated throughout the house, as if long abandonment had **sensitized**[3] its resonance.

Alicia passed the autumn in this strange love nest. She had determined, however, to cast a veil over her former dreams and live like a sleeping beauty in the hostile house, trying not to think about anything until her husband arrived each evening.

It is not strange that she grew thin. She had a light attack of influenza that dragged on **insidiously**[4] for days and days: after that Alicia's health never returned. Finally one afternoon she was able to go into the garden, supported on her husband's arm. She looked around listlessly. Suddenly Jordan, with deep tenderness, ran his hand very slowly over her head, and Alicia instantly burst into sobs, throwing her arms around his neck. For a long time she cried out all the fears she had kept silent, redoubling her weeping at Jordan's slightest caress.

---

[2] friezes—wall paintings or sculptures.

[3] **sensitized**—made sensitive.

[4] **insidiously**—stealthily; with grave results.

Then her sobs subsided, and she stood a long while, her face hidden in the hollow of his neck, not moving or speaking a word.

This was the last day Alicia was well enough to be up. On the following day she awakened feeling faint. Jordan's doctor examined her with minute attention, prescribing calm and absolute rest.

"I don't know," he said to Jordan at the street door. "She has a great weakness that I am unable to explain. And with no vomiting, nothing . . . if she wakes tomorrow as she did today, call me at once. "

When she awakened the following day, Alicia was worse. There was a consultation. It was agreed there was an anemia[5] of incredible progression, completely inexplicable. Alicia had no more fainting spells, but she was visibly moving toward death. The lights were lighted all day long in her bedroom, and there was complete silence. Hours went by without the slightest sound. Alicia dozed. Jordan virtually lived in the drawing room, which was also always lighted. With tireless persistence he paced ceaselessly from one end of the room to the other. The carpet swallowed his steps. At times he entered the bedroom and continued his silent pacing back and forth alongside the bed, stopping for an instant at each end to regard his wife.

Suddenly Alicia began to have hallucinations, vague images, at first seeming to float in the air, then descending to floor level. Her eyes excessively wide, she stared continuously at the carpet on either side of the head of her bed. One night she suddenly focused on one spot. Then she opened her mouth to scream, and pearls of sweat suddenly beaded her nose and lips.

"Jordan! Jordan!" she clamored, rigid with fright, still staring at the carpet.

---

[5] anemia—blood disease causing paleness and weakness.

Jordan ran to the bedroom, and, when she saw him appear, Alicia screamed with terror.

"It's I, Alicia, it's I!"

Alicia looked at him confusedly; she looked at the carpet; she looked at him once again; and after a long moment of stupefied confrontation, she regained her senses. She smiled and took her husband's hand in hers, caressing it, trembling, for half an hour. Among her most persistent hallucinations was that of an **anthropoid**[6] poised on his fingertips on the carpet, staring at her.

The doctors returned, but to no avail. They saw before them a diminishing life, a life bleeding away day by day, hour by hour, absolutely without their knowing why. During their last consultation Alicia lay in a stupor while they took her pulse, passing her inert wrist from one to another. They observed her a long time in silence and then moved into the dining room.

"Phew . . ." The discouraged chief physician shrugged his shoulders. "It is an inexplicable case. There is little we can do . . ."

"That's my last hope!" Jordan groaned. And he staggered blindly against the table.

Alicia's life was fading away in the subdelirium of anemia, a **delirium**[7] which grew worse throughout the evening hours but which let up somewhat after dawn. The illness never worsened during the daytime, but each morning she awakened pale as death, almost in a swoon. It seemed only at night that her life drained out of her in new waves of blood. Always when she awakened she had the sensation of lying collapsed in the bed with a million-pound weight on top of her. Following the third day of this relapse she never left her bed again. She could scarcely move her head. She did not want her bed to be touched, not even to have her bedcovers arranged.

---

[6] **anthropoid**—humanoid; humanlike being.

[7] **delirium**—mental disturbance.

Her **crepuscular**[8] terrors advanced now in the form of monsters that dragged themselves toward the bed and laboriously climbed upon the bedspread.

Then she lost consciousness. The final two days she raved ceaselessly in a weak voice. The lights **funereally**[9] illuminated the bedroom and drawing room. In the deathly silence of the house the only sound was the monotonous delirium from the bedroom and the dull echoes of Jordan's eternal pacing.

Finally, Alicia died. The servant, when she came in afterward to strip the now empty bed, stared wonderingly for a moment at the pillow.

"Sir!" she called Jordan in a low voice. "There are stains on the pillow that look like blood."

Jordan approached rapidly and bent over the pillow. Truly, on the case, on both sides of the hollow left by Alicia's head, were two small dark spots.

"They look like punctures," the servant murmured after a moment of motionless observation.

"Hold it up to the light," Jordan told her.

The servant raised the pillow but immediately dropped it and stood staring at it, livid and trembling. Without knowing why, Jordan felt the hair rise on the back of his neck.

"What is it?" he murmured in a hoarse voice.

"It's very heavy," the servant whispered, still trembling.

Jordan picked it up; it was extraordinarily heavy. He carried it out of the room, and on the dining room table he ripped open the case and the ticking with a slash. The top feathers floated away, and the servant, her mouth opened wide, gave a scream of horror and covered her face with her clenched fists: in the bottom of the pillowcase, among the feathers, slowly moving its hairy

---

[8] **crepuscular**—dusky; shadowy.

[9] **funereally**—suggesting death or a funeral.

legs, was a monstrous animal, a living, **viscous**[10] ball. It was so swollen one could scarcely make out its mouth.

Night after night, since Alicia had taken to her bed, this **abomination**[11] had stealthily applied its mouth— its **proboscis**[12] one might better say—to the girl's temples, sucking her blood. The puncture was scarcely perceptible. The daily plumping of the pillow had doubtlessly at first impeded its progress, but as soon as the girl could no longer move, the suction became **vertiginous.**[13] In five days, in five nights, the monster had drained Alicia's life away.

These parasites of feathered creatures, **diminutive**[14] in their habitual environment, reach enormous proportions under certain conditions. Human blood seems particularly favorable to them, and it is not rare to encounter them in feather pillows.

---

[10] **viscous**—thick and sticky.

[11] **abomination**—disgusting thing.

[12] proboscis—beak; mandible, as with a spider.

[13] **vertiginous**—dizzyingly fast.

[14] **diminutive**—tiny.

QUESTIONS TO CONSIDER

1. Why do you think the author tells the reader that Alicia will die at such an early point in the story?

2. What explanation does the story's last paragraph offer for Alicia's death?

3. If the monster in her pillow was in fact a kind of parasite, why do you think Alicia's hallucinations are of manlike creatures?

Axolotl

BY JULIO CORTÁZAR

Translated by Paul Blackburn

The influential author of the novel Hopscotch, *Julio Cortázar
(Argentina, 1914–1984) was born in Brussels and educated in
Argentina. Despite his early rejection of politics, Cortázar became
an ardent supporter of the Cuban and Nicaraguan revolutions.
As a result of his controversial opinions, however, he lived most of
his life in exile in France. It was there that Cortázar wrote much
of his literature. In his most famous works, "Bestiary," "Continuity
of the Parks," and "Blow Up," he mixes reality and fiction and
explores the relations between life and dreams. These connections
are also clear in "Axolotl."*

    There was a time when I thought a great deal about
the **axolotls**.[1] I went to see them in the aquarium at the
Jardin des Plantes and stayed for hours watching them,
observing their immobility, their faint movements. Now
I am an axolotl.

---

[1] axolotls—Mexican Indian term for salamanders that change shape
and color.

I got to them by chance one spring morning when Paris was spreading its peacock tail after a wintry Lent.[2] I was heading down the boulevard Port-Royal, then I took Saint Marcel and L'Hôpital and saw green among all that grey and remembered the lions. I was friend of the lions and panthers, but had never gone into the dark, humid building that was the aquarium. I left my bike against the gratings and went to look at the tulips. The lions were sad and ugly and my panther was asleep. I decided on the aquarium, looked **obliquely**[3] at banal fish until, unexpectedly, I hit it off with the axolotls. I stayed watching them for an hour and left, unable to think of anything else.

In the library at Sainte-Geneviève, I consulted a dictionary and learned that axolotls are the larval stage (provided with gills) of a species of salamander of the genus Ambystoma. That they were Mexican I knew already by looking at them and their little pink Aztec faces and the placard at the top of the tank. I read that specimens of them had been found in Africa capable of living on dry land during the periods of drought, and continuing their life under water when the rainy season came. I found their Spanish name, *ajolote*, and the mention that they were edible, and that their oil was used (no longer used, it said) like cod-liver oil.

I didn't care to look up any of the specialized works, but the next day I went back to the Jardin des Plantes. I began to go every morning, morning and afternoon some days. The aquarium guard smiled perplexedly taking my ticket. I would lean up against the iron bar in front of the tanks and set to watching them. There's nothing strange in this, because after the first minute I knew that we were linked, that something infinitely lost

---

[2] Lent—in the Christian religion, the season of repentance and prayer that comes before Easter.

[3] **obliquely**—diagonally; at a slant.

and distant kept pulling us together. It had been enough to detain me that first morning in front of the sheet of glass where some bubbles rose through the water. The axolotls huddled on the wretched narrow (only I can know how narrow and wretched) floor of moss and stone in the tank. There were nine specimens, and the majority pressed their heads against the glass, looking with their eyes of gold at whoever came near them. Disconcerted, almost ashamed, I felt it a **lewdness**[4] to be peering at these silent and immobile figures heaped at the bottom of the tank. Mentally I isolated one, situated on the right and somewhat apart from the others, to study it better. I saw a rosy little body, **translucent**[5] (I thought of those Chinese figurines of milky glass), looking like a small lizard about six inches long, ending in a fish's tail of extraordinary delicacy, the most sensitive part of our body. Along the back ran a transparent fin which joined with the tail, but what obsessed me was the feet of the slenderest nicety ending in tiny fingers with minutely human nails. And then I discovered its eyes, its face. Inexpressive features, with no other trait save the eyes, two **orifices**,[6] like brooches, wholly of transparent gold, lacking any life but looking, letting themselves be penetrated by my look, which seemed to travel past the golden level and lose itself in a **diaphanous**[7] interior mystery. A very slender black halo ringed the eye and etched it onto the pink flesh, onto the rosy stone of the head, vaguely triangular, but with curved and irregular sides which gave it a total likeness to a statuette corroded by time. The mouth was masked by the triangular plane of the face, its consider-able size would be guessed only in profile; in front a

---

[4] **lewdness**—vulgarity; an inappropriate thing.

[5] **translucent**—clear; transparent.

[6] **orifices**—openings, especially to a body cavity.

[7] **diaphanous**—sheer; transparent.

delicate crevice barely slit the lifeless stone. On both sides of the head where the ears should have been, there grew three tiny sprigs red as coral, a vegetal outgrowth, the gills, I suppose. And they were the only thing quick about it; every ten or fifteen seconds the sprigs pricked up stiffly and again subsided. Once in a while a foot would barely move, I saw the diminutive toes poise mildly on the moss. It's that we don't enjoy moving a lot, and the tank is so cramped—we barely move in any direction and we're hitting one of the others with our tail or our head—difficulties arise, fights, tiredness. The time feels like it's less if we stay quietly.

It was their quietness that made me lean toward them fascinated the first time I saw the axolotls. Obscurely I seemed to understand their secret will, to abolish space and time with an indifferent immobility. I knew better later; the gill contraction, the tentative reckoning of the delicate feet on the stones, the abrupt swimming (some of them swim with a simple undulation of the body) proved to me that they were capable of escaping that mineral lethargy in which they spent whole hours. Above all else, their eyes obsessed me. In the standing tanks on either side of them, different fishes showed me the simple stupidity of their handsome eyes so similar to our own. The eyes of the axolotls spoke to me of the presence of a different life, of another way of seeing. Glueing my face to the glass (the guard would cough fussily once in a while), I tried to see better those diminutive golden points, that entrance to the infinitely slow and remote world of these rosy creatures. It was useless to tap with one finger on the glass directly in front of their faces; they never gave the least reaction. The golden eyes continued burning with their soft, terrible light; they continued looking at me from an unfathomable depth which made me dizzy.

And nevertheless they were close. I knew it before this, before being an axolotl. I learned it the day I came near them for the first time. The anthropomorphic[8] features of a monkey reveal the reverse of what most people believe, the distance that is traveled from them to us. The absolute lack of similarity between axolotls and human beings proved to me that my recognition was valid, that I was not propping myself up with easy analogies. Only the little hands . . . But an eft, the common newt, has such hands also, and we are not at all alike. I think it was the axolotls' heads, that triangular pink shape with the tiny eyes of gold. That looked and knew. That laid the claim. They were not *animals*.

It would seem easy, almost obvious, to fall into mythology. I began seeing in the axolotls a **metamorphosis**[9] which did not succeed in revoking a mysterious humanity. I imagined them aware, slaves of their bodies, condemned infinitely to the silence of the abyss, to a hopeless meditation. Their blind gaze, the diminutive gold disc without expression and nonetheless terribly shining, went through me like a message: "Save us, save us." I caught myself mumbling words of advice, conveying childish hopes. They continued to look at me, immobile; from time to time the rosy branches of the gills stiffened. In that instant I felt a muted pain; perhaps they were seeing me, attracting my strength to penetrate into the impenetrable thing of their lives. They were not human beings, but I had found in no animal such a profound relation with myself. The axolotls were like witnesses of something, and at times like horrible judges. I felt ignoble in front of them; there was such a terrifying purity in those transparent eyes. They were larvas, but larva means disguise and also phantom.

---

[8] anthropomorphic—humanlike.

[9] **metamorphosis**—transformation.

Behind those Aztec faces, without expression but of an implacable cruelty, what **semblance**[10] was awaiting its hour?

I was afraid of them. I think that had it not been for feeling the proximity of other visitors and the guard, I would not have been bold enough to remain alone with them. "You eat them alive with your eyes, hey," the guard said, laughing; he likely thought I was a little cracked. What he didn't notice was that it was they devouring me slowly with their eyes, in a cannibalism of gold. At any distance from the aquarium, I had only to think of them, it was as though I were being affected from a distance. It got to the point that I was going every day, and at night I thought of them immobile in the darkness, slowly putting a hand out which immediately encountered another. Perhaps their eyes could see in the dead of night, and for them the day continued indefinitely. The eyes of axolotls have no lids.

I know now that there was nothing strange, that that had to occur. Leaning over in front of the tank each morning, the recognition was greater. They were suffering, every fiber of my body reached toward that stifled pain, that stiff torment at the bottom of the tank. They were lying in wait for something, a remote **dominion**[11] destroyed, an age of liberty when the world had been that of the axolotls. Not possible that such a terrible expression which was attaining the overthrow of that forced blankness on their stone faces should carry any message other than one of pain, proof of that eternal sentence, of that liquid hell they were undergoing. Hopelessly, I wanted to prove to myself that my own sensibility was projecting a nonexistent consciousness upon the axolotls. They and I knew. So there was nothing strange in what happened. My face was pressed against

---

[10] **semblance**—unusual thing; appearance.

[11] **dominion**—kingdom or empire.

the glass of the aquarium, my eyes were attempting once more to penetrate the mystery of those eyes of gold without iris, without pupil. I saw from very close up the face of an axolotl immobile next to the glass. No transition and no surprise, I saw my face against the glass, I saw it on the outside of the tank, I saw it on the other side of the glass. Then my face drew back and I understood.

Only one thing was strange: to go on thinking as usual, to know. To realize that was, for the first moment, like the horror of a man buried alive awaking to his fate. Outside, my face came close to the glass again, I saw my mouth, the lips compressed with the effort of understanding the axolotls. I was an axolotl and now I knew instantly that no understanding was possible. He was outside the aquarium, his thinking was a thinking outside the tank. Recognizing him, being him himself, I was an axolotl and in my world. The horror began—I learned in the same moment—of believing myself prisoner in the body of an axolotl, metamorphosed into him with my human mind intact, buried alive in an axolotl, condemned to move lucidly among unconscious creatures. But that stopped when a foot just grazed my face, when I moved just a little to one side and saw an axolotl next to me who was looking at me, and understood that he knew also, no communication possible, but very clearly. Or I was also in him, or all of us were thinking humanlike, incapable of expression, limited to the golden splendor of our eyes looking at the face of the man pressed against the aquarium.

He returned many times, but he comes less often now. Weeks pass without his showing up. I saw him yesterday, he looked at me for a long time and left briskly. It seemed to me that he was not so much interested in us any more, that he was coming out of habit. Since the only thing I do is think, I could think about him a lot. It occurs to me that at the beginning we continued to communicate that he felt more than ever one with the mystery which was claiming him. But the bridges were broken between him and me, because what was his obsession is now an axolotl, alien to his human life. I think that at the beginning I was capable of returning to him in a certain way—ah, only in a certain way—and of keeping awake his desire to know us better. I am an axolotl for good now, and if I think like a man it's only because every axolotl thinks like a man inside his rosy stone semblance. I believe that all this succeeded in communicating something to him in those first days, when I was still he. And in this final solitude to which he no longer comes, I console myself by thinking that perhaps he is going to write a story about us, that, believing he's making up a story, he's going to write all this about axolotls.

QUESTIONS TO CONSIDER

1. What suggestions do you find in the story that the narrator believes axolotls to be precursors of human beings, a kind of earlier stage of conscious existence?

2. What does the narrator mean when he says that for his former self, "his thinking was a thinking outside the tank"?

3. Note that although the narrator states that he is an axolotl, he speaks inconsistently of the axolotls in the tank as "we" and also as "them." Has the narrator become an axolotl after all? If not, what do you think did happen?

4. The narrator makes a point of identifying the axolotls as Mexican, and even as Aztec. What is the significance of this connection?

The Burning Plain

BY JUAN RULFO

Translated by George D. Schade

Somewhat of a recluse, Juan Rulfo (Mexico, 1918–1986) failed to make a deep impression in international literary circles. He is, however, regarded as one of Latin America's most important writers. Rulfo's only publications, a novel entitled Pedro Páramo *and a collection of short stories called* The Burning Plain, *are considered classic pieces of literature. Both publications reflect the tragic consequences of the Mexican Revolution, when death and despair contaminated the lives of the poor. Rulfo paints a gripping portrait of hopelessness in the following story.*

Of the mountains in the south Luvina is the highest and the rockiest. It's infested with that gray stone they make lime from, but in Luvina they don't make lime from it or get any good out of it. They call it crude stone there, and the hill that climbs up toward Luvina they call the Crude Stone Hill. The sun and the air have taken it on themselves to make it crumble away, so that the earth around there is always white and brilliant, as if it were always sparkling with the morning dew, though this is just pure talk, because in Luvina the days are cold as the nights and the dew thickens in the sky before it can fall to the earth.

And the ground is steep and slashed on all sides by deep *barrancas*,[1] so deep you can't make out the bottom. They say in Luvina that one's dreams come up from those *barrancas*; but the only thing I've seen come up out of them was the wind, whistling as if down below they had squeezed it into reed pipes. A wind that doesn't even let the dulcamaras grow: those sad little plants that can live with just a bit of earth, clutching with all their hands at the mountain cliffsides. Only once in a while, where there's a little shade, hidden among the rocks, the chicalote blossoms with its white poppies. But the chicalote soon withers. Then you hear it scratching the air with its spiny branches, making a noise like a knife on a whetstone.

"You'll be seeing that wind that blows over Luvina. It's dark. They say because it's full of volcano sand; anyway, it's a black air. You'll see it. It takes hold of things in Luvina as if it was going to bite them. And there are lots of days when it takes the roofs off the houses as if they were hats, leaving the bare walls uncovered. Then it scratches like it had nails: you hear it morning and night, hour after hour without stopping, scraping the walls, tearing off strips of earth, digging with its sharp shovel under the doors, until you feel it boiling inside of you as if it was going to remove the hinges of your very bones. You'll see."

The man speaking was quiet for a bit, while he looked outside.

The noise of the river reached them, passing its swollen waters through the fig-tree branches, the noise

---

[1] *barrancas*—ravines; gulches.

of the air gently rustling the leaves of the almond trees, and the shouts of the children playing in the small space illumined by the light that came from the store.

The flying ants entered and collided with the oil lamp, falling to the ground with scorched wings. And outside night kept on advancing.

"Hey, Camilo, two more beers!" the man said again. Then he added, "There's another thing, mister. You'll never see a blue sky in Luvina. The whole horizon there is always a dingy color, always clouded over by a dark stain that never goes away. All the hills are bare and treeless, without one green thing to rest your eyes on; everything is wrapped in an ashy smog. You'll see what it's like—those hills silent as if they were dead and Luvina crowning the highest hill with its white houses like a crown of the dead—"

The children's shouts came closer until they penetrated the store. That made the man get up, go to the door and yell at them, "Go away! Don't bother us! Keep on playing, but without so much racket."

Then, coming back to the table, he sat down and said, "Well, as I was saying, it doesn't rain much there. In the middle of the year they get a few storms that whip the earth and tear it away, just leaving nothing but the rocks floating above the stony crust. It's good to see then how the clouds crawl heavily about, how they march from one hill to another jumping as if they were inflated bladders, crashing and thundering just as if they were breaking on the edge of the *barrancas*. But after ten or twelve days they go away and don't come back until the next year, and sometimes they don't come back for several years—No, it doesn't rain much. Hardly at all, so that the earth, besides being all dried up and shriveled like old leather, gets filled with cracks and hard clods of earth like sharp stones, that prick your feet as you walk along, as if the earth itself had grown thorns there. That's what it's like."

He downed his beer, until only bubbles of foam remained in the bottle, then he went on: "Wherever you look in Luvina, it's a very sad place. You're going there, so you'll find out. I would say it's the place where sadness nests. Where smiles are unknown as if people's faces had been frozen. And, if you like, you can see that sadness just any time. The breeze that blows there moves it around but never takes it away. It seems like it was born there. And you can almost taste and feel it, because it's always over you, against you, and because it's heavy like a large plaster weighing on the living flesh of the heart.

"The people from there say that when the moon is full they clearly see the figure of the wind sweeping along Luvina's streets, bearing behind it a black blanket; but what I always managed to see when there was a moon in Luvina was the image of despair—always.

"But drink up your beer. I see you haven't even tasted it. Go ahead and drink. Or maybe you don't like it warm like that. But that's the only kind we have here. I know it tastes bad . . . . Here you get used to it. I swear that there you won't even get this. When you go to Luvina you'll miss it. There all you can drink is a liquor they make from a plant called *hojasé,* and after the first swallows your head'll be whirling around like crazy, feeling like you had banged it against something. So better drink your beer. I know what I'm talking about."

You could still hear the struggle of the river from outside. The noise of the air. The children playing. It seemed to be still early in the evening.

The man had gone once more to the door and then returned, saying: "It's easy to see things, brought back by memory, from here where there's nothing like it. But when it's about Luvina I don't have any trouble going right on talking to you about what I know. I lived there. I left my life there—I went to that place full of illusions and returned old and worn out. And now you're going there—All right. I seem to remember the beginning. I'll put myself in your place and think—Look, when I got to Luvina the first time—But will you let me have a drink of your beer first? I see you aren't paying any attention to it. And it helps me a lot. It relieves me, makes me feel like my head had been rubbed with camphor[2] oil—Well, I was telling you that when I reached Luvina the first time, the mule driver who took us didn't even want to let his animals rest. As soon as he let us off, he turned half around. 'I'm going back,' he said.

"'Wait, aren't you going to let your animals take a rest? They are all worn out.'

"'They'd be in worse shape here,' he said. 'I'd better go back.'

"And away he went, rushing down Crude Stone Hill, spurring his horses on as if he was leaving some place haunted by the devil.

"My wife, my three children, and I stayed there, standing in the middle of the plaza, with all our belongings in our arms. In the middle of that place where all you could hear was the wind.

"Just a plaza, without a single plant to hold back the wind. There we were.

"Then I asked my wife, 'What country are we in, Agripina?'

"And she shrugged her shoulders.

"'Well, if you don't care, go look for a place where we can eat and spend the night. We'll wait for you here,' I told her.

"She took the youngest child by the hand and left. But she didn't come back.

"At nightfall, when the sun was lighting up just the tops of the mountains, we went to look for her. We

---

[2] camphor—aromatic medicinal substance obtained from tree, wood, and bark.

walked along Luvina's narrow streets, until we found her in the church, seated right in the middle of that lonely church, with the child asleep between her legs.

"'What are you doing here, Agripina?'

"'I came in to pray,' she told us.

"'Why?' l asked her.

"She shrugged her shoulders.

"Nobody was there to pray to. It was a vacant old shack without any doors, just some open galleries and a roof full of cracks where the air came through like a sieve.[3]

"'Where's the restaurant?'

"'There isn't any restaurant.'

"'And the inn?'

"'There isn't any inn.'

"'Did you see anybody? Does anybody live here?' I asked her.

"'Yes, there across the street—Some women—I can still see them. Look, there behind the cracks in that door I see some eyes shining, watching us—They have been looking over here—Look at them. I see the shining balls of their eyes—But they don't have anything to give us to eat. They told me without sticking out their heads that there was nothing to eat in this town—Then I came in here to pray, to ask God to help us.'

"'Why didn't you go back to the plaza? We were waiting for you.'

"'I came in here to pray. I haven't finished yet.'

"'What country is this, Agripina?'

"And she shrugged her shoulders again.

"That night we settled down to sleep in a corner of the church behind the dismantled altar. Even there the wind reached, but it wasn't quite as strong. We listened to it passing over us with long howls, we listened to it come in and out of the hollow caves of the doors whipping the

---

[3] sieve—strainer; a device that separates fine particles from coarse ones.

crosses of the stations of the cross[4] with its hands full of air—large rough crosses of mesquite wood hanging from the walls the length of the church, tied together with wires that twanged with each gust of wind like the gnashing of teeth.

"The children cried because they were too scared to sleep. And my wife, trying to hold all of them in her arms. Embracing her handful of children. And me, I didn't know what to do.

"A little before dawn the wind calmed down. Then it returned. But there was a moment during that morning when everything was still, as if the sky had joined the earth, crushing all noise with its weight—You could hear the breathing of the children, who now were resting. I listened to my wife's heavy breath there at my side.

"'What is it?' she said to me.

"'What's what?' I asked her.

"'That, that noise.'

"'It's the silence. Go to sleep. Rest a little bit anyway, because it's going to be day soon.'

"But soon I heard it too. It was like bats flitting through the darkness very close to us. Bats with big wings that grazed against the ground. I got up and the beating of wings was stronger, as if the flock of bats had been frightened and were flying toward the holes of the doors. Then I walked on tiptoes over there, feeling that dull murmur in front of me. I stopped at the door and saw them. I saw all the women of Luvina with their water jugs on their shoulders, their shawls hanging from their heads and their black figures in the black background of the night.

"'What do you want?' I asked them. 'What are you looking for at this time of night?'

"One of them answered, 'We're going for water.'

---

[4] stations of the cross—in Christianity, the 14 crosses or images set up in a church to represent the last sufferings of Jesus.

"I saw them standing in front of me, looking at me. Then, as if they were shadows, they started walking down the street with their black water jugs.

"No, I'll never forget that first night I spent in Luvina.

"Don't you think this deserves another drink? Even if it's just to take away the bad taste of my memories."

* * *

"It seems to me you asked me how many years I was in Luvina, didn't you? The truth is, I don't know. I lost the notion of time since the fevers got it all mixed up for me, but it must have been an eternity—Time is very long there. Nobody counts the hours and nobody cares how the years go mounting up. The days begin and end. Then night comes. Just day and night until the day of death, which for them is a hope.

"You must think I'm **harping**[5] on the same idea. And I am, yes, mister—To be sitting at the threshold of the door, watching the rising and the setting of the sun, raising and lowering your head, until the springs go slack and then everything gets still, timeless, as if you had always lived in eternity. That's what the old folks do there.

"Because only real old folks and those who aren't born yet, as they say, live in Luvina—And weak women, so thin they are just skin and bones. The children born there have all gone away—They hardly see the light of day and they're already grown up. As they say, they jump from their mothers' breast to the hoe and disappear from Luvina. That's the way it is in Luvina.

"There are just old folks left there and lone women, or with a husband who is off God knows where—They appear every now and then when the storms come I was telling you about; you hear a rustling all through

---

[5] **harping**—dwelling; repeating the same idea.

the town when they return and something like a grumbling when they go away again—They leave a sack of provisions for the old folks and plant another child in the bellies of their women, and nobody knows anything more of them until the next year, and sometimes never—It's the custom. There they think that's the way the law is, but it's all the same. The children spend their lives working for their parents as their parents worked for theirs and who knows how many generations back performed this obligation—

"Meanwhile, the old people wait for them and for death, seated in their doorways, their arms hanging slack, moved only by the gratitude of their children— Alone, in that lonely Luvina.

"One day I tried to convince them they should go to another place where the land was good. 'Let's leave here!' I said to them. 'We'll manage somehow to settle somewhere. The government will help us.'

"They listened to me without batting an eyelash, gazing at me from the depths of their eyes from which only a little light came.

"'You say the government will help us, teacher? Do you know the government?'

"I told them I did.

"'We know it too. It just happens. But we don't know anything about the government's mother.'

"I told them it was their country. They shook their heads saying no. And they laughed. It was the only time I saw the people of Luvina laugh. They grinned with their toothless mouths and told me no, that the government didn't have a mother.

"And they're right, you know? That lord only remembers them when one of his boys has done something wrong down here. Then he sends to Luvina for him and they kill him. Aside from that, they don't know if the people exist.

"'You're trying to tell us that we should leave Luvina because you think we've had enough of going hungry without reason,' they said to me. 'But if we leave, who'll bring along our dead ones? They live here and we can't leave them alone.'

"So they're still there. You'll see them now that you're going. Munching on dry mesquite pulp and swallowing their own saliva to keep hunger away. You'll see them pass by like shadows, hugging to the walls of the houses, almost dragged along by the wind.

"'Don't you hear that wind?' I finally said to them. 'It will finish you off.'

"'It keeps on blowing as long as it ought to. It's God's will,' they answered me. 'It's bad when it stops blowing. When that happens the sun pours into Luvina and sucks our blood and the little bit of moisture we have in our skin. The wind keeps the sun up above. It's better that way.'

"So I didn't say anything else to them. I left Luvina and I haven't gone back and I don't intend to.

"—But look at the way the world keeps turning. You're going there now in a few hours. Maybe it's been fifteen years since they said the same thing to me: 'You're going to San Juan Luvina.'

"In those days I was strong. I was full of ideas—You know how we're all full of ideas. And one goes with the idea of making something of them everywhere. But it didn't work out in Luvina. I made the experiment and it failed—

"San Juan Luvina. That name sounded to me like a name in the heavens. But it's purgatory.[6] A dying place where even the dogs have died off, so there's not a creature to bark at the silence; for as soon as you get

---

[6] purgatory—in Roman Catholicism, a place, neither heaven nor hell, where souls repent for their sins.

used to the strong wind that blows there all you hear is the silence that reigns in these lonely parts. And that gets you down. Just look at me. What it did to me. You're going there, so you'll soon understand what I mean—

"What do you say we ask this fellow to pour a little mescal?[7] With this beer you have to get up and go all the time and that interrupts our talk a lot. Hey, Camilo, let's have two mescals this time!

"Well, now, as I was telling you—"

But he didn't say anything. He kept staring at a fixed point on the table where the flying ants, now wingless, circled about like naked worms.

Outside you could hear the night advancing. The lap of the water against the fig-tree trunks. The children's shouting, now far away. The stars peering through the small hole of the door.

The man who was staring at the flying ants slumped over the table and fell asleep.

---

[7] mescal—Mexican liquor.

QUESTIONS TO CONSIDER

1. What aspects of day-to-day life in Mexico are reflected in this story?

2. What do you think made the old people of Luvina laugh so unexpectedly at the storyteller?

3. What might explain the attitude of the people of Luvina?

The Third Bank of the River

BY JOÃO GUIMARÃES ROSA

Translated by Barbara Shelby

João Guimarães Rosa (Brazil, 1908–1967) was born in Minas Gerais, which borders Brazil's vast and isolated backlands of plain and jungle. A man of many talents, he practiced medicine, served as a delegate to UNESCO, and produced an impressive collection of literature. Guimarães Rosa's most significant work is The Devil to Pay in the Backlands, *which, like much of his fiction, takes place in the Brazilian backlands. In "The Third Bank of the River," a father's abandonment of his family raises questions about the conflict between personal happiness and duty to others.*

My father was a dutiful, orderly, straightforward man. And according to several reliable people of whom I inquired, he had had these qualities since adolescence or even childhood. By my own recollection, he was neither jollier nor more melancholy than the other men we knew. Maybe a little quieter. It was mother, not father, who ruled the house. She scolded us daily—my sister, my brother, and me. But it happened one day that father ordered a boat.

He was very serious about it. It was to be made specially for him, of mimosa wood. It was to be sturdy enough to last twenty or thirty years and just large enough for one person. Mother carried on plenty about it. Was her husband going to become a fisherman all of a sudden? Or a hunter? Father said nothing. Our house was less than a mile from the river, which around there was deep, quiet, and so wide you couldn't see across it.

I can never forget the day the rowboat was delivered. Father showed no joy or other emotion. He just put on his hat as he always did and said goodbye to us. He took along no food or bundle of any sort. We expected mother to rant and rave, but she didn't. She looked very pale and bit her lip, but all she said was:

"If you go away, stay away. Don't ever come back!"

Father made no reply. He looked gently at me and motioned me to walk along with him. I feared mother's wrath, yet I eagerly obeyed. We headed toward the river together. I felt bold and exhilarated, so much so that I said:

"Father, will you take me with you in your boat?"

He just looked at me, gave me his blessing, and, by a gesture, told me to go back. I made as if to do so but, when his back was turned, I ducked behind some bushes to watch him. Father got into the boat and rowed away. Its shadow slid across the water like a crocodile, long and quiet.

Father did not come back. Nor did he go anywhere, really. He just rowed and floated across and around, out there in the river. Everyone was appalled. What had never happened, what could not possibly happen, was happening. Our relatives, neighbors, and friends came over to discuss the phenomenon.

Mother was ashamed. She said little and conducted herself with great **composure**.[1] As a consequence, almost everyone thought (though no one said it) that father had gone insane. A few, however, suggested that father might be fulfilling a promise he had made to God or to a saint, or that he might have some horrible disease, maybe leprosy, and that he left for the sake of the family, at the same time wishing to remain fairly near them.

Travelers along the river and people living near the bank on one side or the other reported that father never put foot on land, by day or night. He just moved about on the river, solitary, aimless, like a **derelict**.[2] Mother and our relatives agreed that the food which he had doubtless hidden in the boat would soon give out and that then he would either leave the river and travel off somewhere (which would be at least a little more respectable) or he would repent and come home.

How far from the truth they were! Father had a secret source of provisions: me. Every day I stole food and brought it to him. The first night after he left, we all lit fires on the shore and prayed and called to him. I was deeply distressed and felt a need to do something more. The following day I went down to the river with a loaf of corn bread, a bunch of bananas, and some bricks of raw brown sugar. I waited impatiently a long, long hour. Then I saw the boat, far off, alone, gliding almost imperceptibly on the smoothness of the river. Father was sitting in the bottom of the boat. He saw me but he did not row toward me or make any gesture. I showed him the food and then I placed it in a hollow rock on the river bank; it was safe there from animals, rain, and

---

[1] **composure**—calmness; self-possession.

[2] **derelict**—homeless person.

dew. I did this day after day, on and on and on. Later I learned, to my surprise, that mother knew what I was doing and left food around where I could easily steal it. She had a lot of feelings she didn't show.

Mother sent for her brother to come and help on the farm and in business matters. She had the schoolteacher come and tutor us children at home because of the time we had lost. One day, at her request, the priest put on his vestments, went down to the shore, and tried to exorcise[3] the devils that had got into my father. He shouted that father had a duty to cease his unholy obstinacy. Another day she arranged to have two soldiers come and try to frighten him. All to no avail. My father went by in the distance, sometimes so far away he could barely be seen. He never replied to anyone and no one ever got close to him. When some newspapermen came in a launch to take his picture, father headed his boat to the other side of the river and into the marshes, which he knew like the palm of his hand but in which other people quickly got lost. There in his private maze, which extended for miles, with heavy foliage overhead and rushes on all sides, he was safe.

We had to get accustomed to the idea of father's being out on the river. We had to but we couldn't, we never could. I think I was the only one who understood to some degree what our father wanted and what he did not want. The thing I could not understand at all was how he stood the hardship. Day and night, in sun and rain, in heat and in the terrible midyear cold spells, with his old hat on his head and very little other clothing, week after week, month after month, year after year, **unheedful**[4] of the waste and emptiness in which his life was slipping by. He never set foot on earth or grass, on isle or mainland shore. No doubt he sometimes tied up

---

[3] exorcise—expel evil spirits through command or prayer.

[4] **unheedful**—paying no attention to.

the boat at a secret place, perhaps at the tip of some island, to get a little sleep. He never lit a fire or even struck a match and he had no flashlight. He took only a small part of the food that I left in the hollow rock—not enough, it seemed to me, for survival. What could his state of health have been? How about the continual drain on his energy, pulling and pushing the oars to control the boat? And how did he survive the annual floods, when the river rose and swept along with it all sorts of dangerous objects—branches of trees, dead bodies of animals—that might suddenly crash against his little boat?

He never talked to a living soul. And we never talked about him. We just thought. No, we could never put our father out of mind. If for a short time we seemed to, it was just a lull from which we would be sharply awakened by the realization of his frightening situation.

My sister got married, but mother didn't want a wedding party. It would have been a sad affair, for we thought of him every time we ate some especially tasty food. Just as we thought of him in our cozy beds on a cold, stormy night—out there, alone and unprotected, trying to bail out the boat with only his hands and a gourd.[5] Now and then someone would say that I was getting to look more and more like my father. But I knew that by then his hair and beard must have been shaggy and his nails long. I pictured him thin and sickly, black with hair and sunburn, and almost naked despite the articles of clothing I occasionally left for him.

He didn't seem to care about us at all. But I felt affection and respect for him, and, whenever they praised me because I had done something good, I said:

"My father taught me to act that way."

It wasn't exactly accurate but it was a truthful sort of lie. As I said, father didn't seem to care about us. But

---

[5] gourd—dried and hollowed-out shell of a fruit.

then why did he stay around there? Why didn't he go up the river or down the river, beyond the possibility of seeing us or being seen by us? He alone knew the answer.

My sister had a baby boy. She insisted on showing father his grandson. One beautiful day we all went down to the river bank, my sister in her white wedding dress, and she lifted the baby high. Her husband held a parasol above them. We shouted to father and waited. He did not appear. My sister cried; we all cried in each other's arms.

My sister and her husband moved far away. My brother went to live in a city. Times changed, with their usual imperceptible rapidity. Mother finally moved too; she was old and went to live with her daughter. I remained behind, a leftover. I could never think of marrying. I just stayed there with the **impedimenta**[6] of my life. Father, wandering alone and **forlorn**[7] on the river, needed me. I knew he needed me, although he never even told me why he was doing it. When I put the question to people bluntly and insistently, all they told me was that they heard that father had explained it to the man who made the boat. But now this man was dead and nobody knew or remembered anything. There was just some foolish talk, when the rains were especially severe and persistent, that my father was wise like Noah and had the boat built in anticipation of a new flood; I dimly remember people saying this. In any case, I would not condemn my father for what he was doing. My hair was beginning to turn gray.

I have only sad things to say. What bad had I done, what was my great guilt? My father always away and his absence always with me. And the river, always the river, perpetually renewing itself. The river, always. I

---

[6] **impedimenta**—burdens.

[7] **forlorn**—sad and hopeless.

was beginning to suffer from old age, in which life is just a sort of lingering. I had attacks of illness and of anxiety. I had a nagging rheumatism.[8] And he? Why, why was he doing it? He must have been suffering terribly. He was so old. One day, in his failing strength, he might let the boat capsize; or he might let the current carry it downstream, on and on, until it plunged over the waterfall to the boiling turmoil below. It pressed upon my heart. He was out there and I was forever robbed of my peace. I am guilty of I know not what, and my pain is an open wound inside me. Perhaps I would know—if things were different. I began to guess what was wrong.

Out with it! Had I gone crazy? No, in our house that word was never spoken, never through all the years. No one called anybody crazy, for nobody is crazy. Or maybe everybody. All I did was go there and wave a handkerchief. So he would be more likely to see me. I was in complete command of myself. I waited. Finally he appeared in the distance, there, then over there, a vague shape sitting in the back of the boat. I called to him several times. And I said what I was so eager to say, to state formally and under oath. I said it as loud as I could:

"Father, you have been out there long enough. You are old . . . Come back, you don't have to do it anymore . . . Come back and I'll go instead. Right now, if you want. Any time. I'll get into the boat. I'll take your place."

And when I had said this my heart beat more firmly.

He heard me. He stood up. He maneuvered with his oars and headed the boat toward me. He had accepted my offer. And suddenly I trembled, down deep. For he had raised his arm and waved—the first time in so many, so many years. And I couldn't. . . . In terror, my

---

[8] rheumatism—condition characterized by pain in the muscles and joints.

hair on end, I ran, I fled madly. For he seemed to come from another world. And I'm begging forgiveness, begging, begging.

I experienced the dreadful sense of cold that comes from deadly fear, and I became ill. Nobody ever saw or heard about him again. Am I a man, after such a failure? I am what never should have been. I am what must be silent. I know it is too late. I must stay in the deserts and unmarked plains of my life, and I fear I shall shorten it. But when death comes I want them to take me and put me in a little boat in this perpetual water between the long shores; and I, down the river, lost in the river, inside the river . . . the river . . .

QUESTIONS TO CONSIDER

1. Why is this tale more than a story about a man escaping from an unhappy life?

2. The narrator describes his father's life on the river as "aimless." Do you agree? What do you think he feels he is accomplishing on the river?

3. If the father does not seem to care about his family any longer, why is his son so careful to give his father credit for having raised him well?

4. How, if at all, does the narrator fail his father?

The Eclipse

BY AUGUSTO MONTERROSO

Translated by Edith Grossman

Honduran by birth, Augusto Monterroso (Guatemala, 1921–) grew up in Guatemala. His vehement opposition to that country's political regime forced him to flee to Mexico. Although he has also worked as a diplomat, Monterroso does not advance a political agenda in his literature. In fact, he is mostly known for writing meticulously and concisely. His succinct style is nowhere more evident than in the one-line essay, "Fecundity." In this clever story, Monterroso describes an encounter between a proud Spanish monk and the native people who are about to kill him.

When Brother Bartolomé Arrazola felt that he was lost, he accepted the fact that now nothing could save him. The powerful jungle of Guatemala, implacable and final, had overwhelmed him. In the face of his **topographical**[1] ignorance he sat down calmly to wait for death. He wanted to die there, without hope, alone, his

---

[1] **topographical**—geographical; territorial.

thoughts fixed on distant Spain, particularly on the Convent of Los Abrojos, where Charles V had once condescended to come down from his **eminence**[2] to tell him that he trusted in the religious zeal of his work of redemption.

When he awoke he found himself surrounded by a group of Indians with impassive faces who were preparing to sacrifice him before an altar, an altar that seemed to Bartolomé the bed on which he would finally rest from his fears, from his destiny, from himself.

Three years in the country had given him a passing knowledge of the native languages. He tried something. He spoke a few words that were understood.

Then there blossomed in him an idea which he considered worthy of his talent and his broad education and his profound knowledge of Aristotle.[3] He remembered that a total eclipse of the sun was to take place that day. And he decided, in the deepest part of his being, to use that knowledge to deceive his oppressors and save his life.

"If you kill me," he said, "I can make the sun darken on high."

The Indians stared at him and Bartolomé caught the disbelief in their eyes. He saw them consult with one another and he waited confidently, not without a certain contempt.

Two hours later the heart of Brother Bartolomé Arrazola spurted out its passionate blood on the sacrificing stone (brilliant in the opaque light of the eclipsed sun) while one of the Indians recited tonelessly, slowly, one by one, the infinite list of dates when solar and lunar eclipses would take place, which the

---

[2] **eminence**—highness; distinction.

[3] Aristotle—ancient Greek philosopher.

astronomers of the Mayan community had predicted and registered in their **codices**[4] without the **estimable**[5] help of Aristotle.

---

[4] **codices**—ancient book manuscripts.

[5] **estimable**—admirable; esteemed.

QUESTIONS TO CONSIDER

1. For what purpose has Brother Bartolomé come to Guatemala? Of what do you think "his talent and his broad education" are likely to have consisted?

2. What do you think the author believes accounts for Brother Bartolomé's contempt for the native peoples of Guatemala?

3. In what way might this story be described as a fable?

Bottles

BY ALCINA LUBITCH DOMECQ

Translated by Ilan Stavans

Alcina Lubitch Domecq (Guatemala, 1953–) is a remarkable Spanish-speaking Jewish writer. Forced to flee her native country as a result of family feuds and economic instability, she emigrated to Israel. There Lubitch Domecq studied at Hebrew University and worked as a business consultant while writing stories. Her two published books are the collection Intoxicada *and the novel* El espejo en el espejo: o La noble sonrisa del perro. *In "Bottles," a young girl describes her mother's mental decay and gradual isolation from the family.*

Mom was taken away, I don't know exactly where. Dad says she is in a nice place where they take good care of her. I miss her . . . although I understand. Dad says she suffered from a sickening love for bottles. First she started to buy them in the supermarket. All sorts of bottles—plastic and crystal, small and big. Everything had to be packed in a bottle—noodle soup, lemon juice, bathroom soap, pencils. She just wouldn't buy something that wasn't in one. Dad complained. Sometimes that was the reason we wouldn't have toilet paper, or there wouldn't be any salt. And Mom used to kiss the bottles all day long. She polished them with great affection, talked to them, and at times I remember her saying she was going to eat one. You could open a kitchen cabinet and find a million bottles. A million. I hated them, and so did my sister. I mean, why store the dirty linen in a huge bottle the size of a garbage can? Dad says Mom didn't know anything about logic. I remember one night, after dinner, when Mom apologized and left in a hurry. An hour later she returned with a box full of wine bottles. Dad asked her what had got into her. She said she had been at the liquor store, and immediately started to empty every single bottle into the toilet. All the wine was dumped. She just needed the bottles. Dad and I and my sister just sat there, on the living room couch, watching Mom wash and kiss those ugly wine bottles. I think my sister began to cry. But Mom didn't care. Then Dad called the police but they didn't do a thing. Weeks later, we pretended to have forgotten everything. It was then that Mom began screaming that she was pregnant, like when my sister was born. She was shouting that a tiny plastic bottle was living inside her stomach. She said she was having pain. She was vomiting and pale. She cried a lot. Dad called an ambulance and Mom was taken to the hospital. There the doctors made X-rays and checked her all over. Nothing was wrong. They just couldn't find the tiny plastic bottle. But for days she kept insisting that it was living inside her, growing; that's what she used to say to me and my sister. Not to Dad anymore, because he wouldn't listen to her, he just wouldn't listen. I miss Mom. . . . She was taken away a month later, after the event with the statue in the living room. You see, one afternoon she decided that the tiny bottle wasn't in her stomach anymore. Now she felt bad because something was going to happen to her. Like a prophecy. She was feeling that something was coming upon her. And next morning, before my sister and I left for school, we found Mom near the couch, standing in the living room. She was vertical, standing straight. She couldn't walk around. Like in a cell. I asked her why she wouldn't move, why she wouldn't go to the kitchen or to my room. Mom answered that she couldn't because she was trapped in a bottle, a gigantic one. We could see her and she could see us too, but according to Mom, nobody could touch her body because there was glass surrounding it. Actually, I touched her and I never felt any glass. Neither did Dad or my sister. But Mom insisted that she couldn't feel us. For days she stayed in that position, and after some time I was able to picture the big bottle. Mom was like a spider you catch in the back yard and suffocate in Tupperware. That's when the ambulance came for the second time. I wasn't home, but Dad was. He was there when they took her away. I was at school, although I knew what was happening. That same day we threw away all the bottles in a nearby dump. The neighbors were staring at us but we didn't care. It felt good, very good.

QUESTIONS TO CONSIDER

1. "Mom was like a spider you catch in the backyard and suffocate in Tupperware." What does this quote suggest about the family's relationship with Mom?

2. How might this story be read as a metaphor for isolation?

Land of Contrasts

A view of the centuries-old Catholic University of Chile and of modern-day Santiago.

◄ Oil drills are exemplary
of Latin America's growing
petroleum industry.

▲
The busy streets of Bogotá show the bustle of a rapidly developing city.

◀ A man plows his field in Colombia the traditional way—without
the use of machinery.

Bosques de las Lomas, an affluent housing complex in Mexico City.

A wealthy family in Bogotá, Colombia.

An impoverished area in northeastern Brasília.

A man sorting through garbage and a woman washing dishes in one of the poorest parts of eastern Brazil.

▲
A lush forest in the Sierra Nevada de Santa Marta in Colombia.

Wild horses running across the dry Argentine pampas.

The bottom of a canyon in the mountainous part of Chiapas, Mexico.

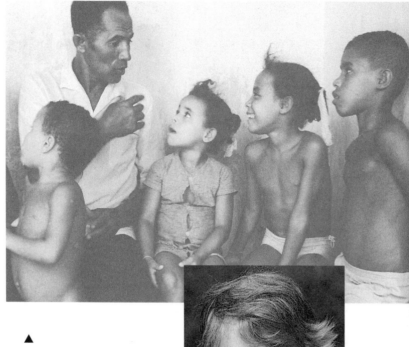

▲
A fisherman in Brazil
telling his children a story.

An Argentine businessman
of Italian origin. ▶

◀ A religious procession
during Holy Week.

▲
A traditionally dressed Indian from Ecuador.

chapter 4

Authenticity and Redemption

The Secret Miracle

BY JORGE LUIS BORGES

Translated by Andrew Hurley

Jorge Luis Borges (Argentina, 1899–1986) is regarded as one of the most influential writers of the 20th century. His numerous poems, essays, and short stories are widely studied and acclaimed, noted especially for their originality and philosophical tint. Borges is most famous for writing about time and its infinite possibilities, a theme he explores in detail in the following selection.

> *And God caused him to die for a hundred years, and then raised him to life. And God said, "How long hast thou waited?" He said, "I have waited a day or part of a day."*
> Qur'ān, 2:261p,

On the night of March 14, 1939, in an apartment on Prague's Zeltnergasse, Jaromir Hladik, author of the unfinished tragedy *The Enemies*, a book titled *A Vindication of Eternity*, and a study of Jakob Boehme's indirect Jewish sources, dreamed of a long game of chess. The game was played not by two individuals, but by two illustrious families; it had been started many centuries in the past. No one could say what the forgotten prize was to be, but it was rumored to be vast, perhaps even infinite. The chess pieces and the chess-board themselves were in a secret tower. Jaromir (in the dream) was the firstborn son of one of the contending families; the clocks chimed the hour of the inescapable game; the dreamer was running across the sand of a desert in the rain, but he could recall neither the figures nor the rules of chess. At that point, Hladik awoke. The din of the rain and the terrible clocks ceased. A rhythmic and unanimous sound, punctuated by the barking of orders, rose from the Zeltnergasse. It was sunrise, and the armored vanguard of the Third Reich[1] was rolling into Prague.

On the nineteenth, the authorities received a report from an informer. That same day, toward dusk, Jaromir Hladik was arrested. He was led to a white, **aseptic**[2] jail on the opposite bank of the Moldau. He was unable to refute even one of the Gestapo's[3] charges: His mother's family's name was Jaroslavski, he came of Jewish blood, his article on Boehme dealt with a Jewish subject, his was one of the accusing signatures appended to a protest against the Anschluss. In 1928, he had translated the *Sefer Yetsirah* for Hermann Barsdorf Publishers; that company's effusive catalog had exaggerated (as commercial catalogs do) the translator's renown; the catalog had been **perused**[4] by Capt. Julius Rothe, one of the officers in whose hands his fate now lay. There is no one who outside his own area of knowledge is

---

[1] Third Reich—Hitler's totalitarian regime in Nazi Germany during World War II.

[2] **aseptic**—stark; cold.

[3] Gestapo's—belonging to internal security police of Nazi Germany, which was known for its terrorist methods.

[4] **perused**—read; examined carefully.

not **credulous;**[5] two or three adjectives in Fraktur were enough to persuade Julius Rothe of Hladik's preeminence, and therefore that he should be put to death—*pour encourager les autres.*[6] The date was set for March 29, at 9:00 A.M. That delay (whose importance the reader will soon discover) was caused by the administrative desire to work impersonally and deliberately, as vegetables do, or planets.

Hladik's first emotion was simple terror. He reflected that he wouldn't have **quailed**[7] at being hanged, or decapitated, or having his throat slit, but being shot by a firing squad was unbearable. In vain he told himself a thousand times that the pure and universal act of dying was what ought to strike fear, not the concrete circumstances of it, and yet Hladik never wearied of picturing to himself those circumstances. Absurdly, he tried to foresee every variation. He anticipated the process endlessly, from the sleepless dawn to the mysterious discharge of the rifles. Long before the day that Julius Rothe had set, Hladik died hundreds of deaths— standing in courtyards whose shapes and angles ran the entire gamut of geometry, shot down by soldiers of changing faces and varying numbers who sometimes took aim at him from afar, sometimes from quite near. He faced his imaginary executions with true fear, perhaps with true courage. Each enactment lasted several seconds; when the circle was closed, Hladik would return, unendingly, to the shivering eve of his death. Then it occurred to him that reality seldom coincides with the way we envision it beforehand; he inferred, with perverse logic, that to foresee any particular detail is in fact to prevent its happening. Trusting in that frail magic, he began to invent horrible details—*so that they would not occur;* naturally he wound up fearing that

---

[5] **credulous**—gullible; easily convinced.

[6] *pour encourager les autres*—as an example to others.

[7] **quailed**—shrunk back in fear.

those details might be prophetic. Miserable in the night, he tried to **buttress**[8] his courage somehow on the fleeting stuff of time. He knew that time was rushing toward the morning of March 29; he reasoned aloud: *It is now the night of the twenty-second, so long as this night and six more last I am invulnerable, immortal.* He mused that the nights he slept were deep, dim cisterns into which he could sink. Sometimes, impatiently, he yearned for the shots that would end his life once and for all, the blast that would redeem him, for good or ill, from his vain imaginings. On the twenty-eighth, as the last rays of the sun were glimmering on the high bars of his window, he was diverted from those abject thoughts by the image of his play, *The Enemies*.

Hladik was past forty. Apart from a few friends and many routines, the problematic pursuit of literature constituted the whole of his life; like every writer, he measured other men's virtues by what they had accomplished, yet asked that other men measure him by what he planned someday to do. All the books he had sent to the press left him with complex regret. Into his articles on the work of Boehme, Ibn Ezra, and Fludd, he had poured mere diligence, application; into his translation of the *Sefer Yetsirah*, oversight, weariness, and conjecture. He judged *A Vindication of Eternity* to be less unsatisfactory, perhaps. The first volume documents the diverse eternities that mankind has invented, from Parmenides' static Being to Hinton's modifiable past; the second denies (with Francis Bradley) that all the events of the universe constitute a *temporal*[9] series. It argues that the number of humankind's possible experiences is not infinite, and that a single "repetition" is sufficient to prove that time is a fallacy. . . . Unfortunately, no less fallacious are the arguments that prove that fallacy; Hladik was in the habit of ticking

---

[8] **buttress**—support.

[9] *temporal*—chronological.

them off with a certain disdainful perplexity. He had also drafted a cycle of expressionist poems; these, to the poet's confusion, appeared in a 1924 anthology and there was never a subsequent anthology that didn't inherit them. With his verse drama *The Enemies*, Hladik believed he could redeem himself from all that equivocal and **languid**[10] past. (He admired verse in drama because it does not allow the spectators to forget unreality, which is a condition of art.)

This play observed the unities of time, place, and action; it took place in Hradcany, in the library of Baron Römerstadt on one of the last evenings of the nineteenth century. In Act 1, Scene I, a stranger pays a visit to Römerstadt. (A clock strikes seven, a vehemence of last sunlight exalts the windowpanes, on a breeze float the ecstatic notes of a familiar Hungarian melody.) This visit is followed by others; the persons who come to **importune**[11] Römerstadt are strangers to him, though he has the uneasy sense that he has seen them before, perhaps in a dream. All fawn upon him, but it is clear— first to the play's audience, then to the baron himself— that they are secret enemies, sworn to his destruction. Römerstadt manages to check or fend off their complex intrigues; in the dialogue they allude to his fiancée, Julia de Weidenau, and to one Jaroslav Kubin, who once importuned her with his love. Kubin has now gone mad, and believes himself to be Römerstadt. . . . The dangers mount; by the end of the second act, Römerstadt finds himself forced to kill one of the conspirators. Then the third and last act begins. Little by little, incoherencies multiply; actors come back onstage who had apparently been discarded from the plot; for one instant, the man that Römerstadt killed returns. Someone points out that the hour has grown no later:

---

[10] **languid**—spiritless.
[11] **importune**—plead with.

the clock strikes seven; upon the high windowpanes the western sunlight shimmers; the thrilling Hungarian melody floats upon the air. The first **interlocutor**[12] comes onstage again and repeats the same words he spoke in Act I, Scene 1. Without the least surprise or astonishment, Römerstadt talks with him; the audience realizes that Römerstadt is the pitiable Jaroslav Kubin. The play has not taken place; it is the circular delirium that Kubin endlessly experiences and reexperiences.

Hladik had never asked himself whether this tragicomedy of errors was banal or admirable, carefully plotted or accidental. In the design I have outlined here, he had **intuitively**[13] hit upon the best way of hiding his shortcomings and giving full play to his strengths, the possibility of rescuing (albeit symbolically) that which was fundamental to his life. He had finished the first act and one or another scene of the third; the metrical nature of the play allowed him to go over it continually, correcting the hexameters,[14] without a manuscript. It occurred to him that he still had two acts to go, yet very soon he was to die. In the darkness he spoke with God. *If*, he prayed, *I do somehow exist, if I am not one of Thy repetitions or errata, then I exist as the author of* The Enemies. *In order to complete that play, which can justify me and justify Thee as well, I need one more year. Grant me those days, Thou who art the centuries and time itself.* It was the last night, the most monstrous night, but ten minutes later sleep flooded Hladik like some dark ocean.

Toward dawn, he dreamed that he was in hiding, in one of the naves of the Clementine Library. *What are you looking for?* a librarian wearing dark glasses asked him. *I'm looking for God*, Hladik replied. *God*, the librarian said, *is in one of the letters on one of the pages of one of the four hundred thousand volumes in the Clementine. My*

---

[12] **interlocutor**—person who takes part in a conversation.

[13] **intuitively**—knowingly.

[14] hexameters—lines of verse consisting of six metrical feet.

parents and my parents' parents searched for that letter; I myself have gone blind searching for it. He removed his spectacles and Hladik saw his eyes, which were dead. A reader came in to return an atlas. This atlas is worthless, he said, and handed it to Hladik. Hladik opened it at random. He saw a map of India—a dizzying page. Suddenly certain, he touched one of the tiny letters. A voice that was everywhere spoke to him: The time for your labor has been granted. Here Hladik awoke.

He remembered that the dreams of men belong to God and that Maimonides had written that the words of a dream, when they are dear and distinct and one cannot see who spoke them, are holy. Hladik put his clothes on; two soldiers entered the cell and ordered him to follow them.

From inside his cell, Hladik had thought that when he emerged he would see a maze of galleries, stairways, and wings. Reality was not so rich; he and the soldiers made their way down a single iron staircase into a rear yard. Several soldiers—some with their uniforms unbuttoned—were looking over a motorcycle, arguing about it. The sergeant looked at his watch; it was eight forty-four. They had to wait until nine. Hladik, feeling more insignificant than ill fortuned, sat down on a pile of firewood. He noticed that the soldiers' eyes avoided his own. To make the wait easier, the sergeant handed him a cigarette. Hladik did not smoke; he accepted the cigarette out of courtesy, or out of humility. When he lighted it, he saw that his hands were trembling. The day clouded over; the soldiers were speaking in low voices, as though he were already dead. Vainly he tried to recall the woman that Julia de Weidenau had symbolized. . . .

The firing squad fell in, lined up straight. Hladik, standing against the prison wall, awaited the discharge. Someone was afraid the wall would be spattered with blood; the prisoner was ordered to come forward a few steps. Absurdly, Hladik was reminded of the preliminary shufflings-about of photographers. A heavy drop of rain grazed Hladik's temple and rolled slowly down his cheek; the sergeant called out the final order.

The physical universe stopped.

The weapons converged upon Hladik, but the men who were to kill him were immobile. The sergeant's arm seemed to freeze, eternal, in an inconclusive gesture. On one of the paving stones of the yard, a bee cast a motionless shadow. As though in a painting, the wind had died. Hladik attempted a scream, a syllable, the twisting of a hand. He realized that he was paralyzed. He could hear not the slightest murmur of the halted world. *I am in hell*, he thought, *I am dead*. Then *I am mad*, he thought. And then, *time has halted*. Then he reflected that if that were true, his thoughts would have halted as well. He tried to test this conjecture: he repeated (without moving his lips) Virgil's mysterious fourth eclogue. He imagined that the now remote soldiers must be as disturbed by this as he was; he wished he could communicate with them. He was surprised and puzzled to feel neither the slightest weariness nor any faintness from his long immobility. After an indeterminate time, he slept. When he awoke, the world was still motionless and muffled. The drop of water still hung on his cheek; on the yard, there still hung the shadow of the bee; in the air the smoke from the cigarette he'd smoked had never **wafted**[15] away. Another of those "days" passed before Hladik understood.

He had asked God for an entire year in which to finish his work; God in His **omnipotence**[16] had granted him a year. God had performed for him a secret miracle: the German bullet would kill him, at the determined hour, but in Hladik's mind a year would pass between

---

[15] **wafted**—drifted.

[16] **omnipotence**—unlimited power.

the order to fire and the discharge of the rifles. From perplexity Hladik moved to stupor, from stupor to resignation, from resignation to sudden gratitude.

He had no document but his memory; the fact that he had to learn each hexameter as he added it imposed upon him a providential strictness, unsuspected by those who essay and then forget vague provisional paragraphs. He did not work for posterity, nor did he work for God, whose literary preferences were largely unknown to him. Painstakingly, motionlessly, secretly, he forged in time his grand invisible labyrinth. He redid the third act twice. He struck out one and another overly obvious symbol—the repeated chimings of the clock, the music. No detail was irksome to him. He cut, condensed, expanded; in some cases he decided the original version should stand. He came to love the courtyard, the prison; one of the faces that stood before him altered his conception of Römerstadt's character. He discovered that the hard-won **cacophonies**[17] that were so alarming to Flaubert are mere visual superstitions—weaknesses and irritations of the written, not the sounded, word. . . . He completed his play; only a single epithet was left to be decided upon now. He found it; the drop of water rolled down his cheek. He began a maddened cry, he shook his head, and the fourfold volley **felled**[18] him.

Jaromir Hladik died on the twenty-ninth of March, at 9:02 A.M.

---

[17] **cacophonies**—harsh sounds.

[18] **felled**—killed.

QUESTIONS TO CONSIDER

1. Who is Jaromir Hladik? Why is he arrested?

2. Why doesn't Hladik imagine all of the ways he may be killed?

3. What is Hladik's play, *The Enemies*, about? Why is its content significant to this story?

4. Why does Hladik's miracle have to be a secret?

A Heaven
Without Crows

BY ILAN STAVANS

Ilan Stavans (Mexico, 1961–) is internationally known as a multi-lingual author, writing with equal ease in Yiddish, Spanish, and English. In addition to having written many short stories, Stavans has published essays, most notable of which are The Hispanic Condition *and* The Riddle of Cantinflas. *In "A Heaven Without Crows," Stavans uses a fictitious letter to explain a true part of history—Franz Kafka's request that his writing be destroyed. Kafka was a Czech writer who combined realistic details with fantastic, dreamlike images in his work. His friend, Max Brod, ignored his request to burn his writings and published them instead.*

2 1, V, 1924,
Kierling Sanatorium
Klosterneuberg

Dear Max,

Thanks for having come ten days ago to visit the old invalid who's about to say goodbye. Just a few miles from Vienna and already I feel I'm in the Other World. I have tuberculosis in the larynx, I know, though the doctors persist in offering other diagnoses, incredible beyond belief. Why won't anyone dare to talk honestly to a dying man? Death is the issue and still they're vague, evasive. Dr. Tschiassny tells me that my throat is looking much better but I don't believe him; I can't even swallow solid food any more, so I live on lemonade, beer, wine, and water. They apply ice packs to my throat on a regular basis. I've also been given medicated lozenges and Demropon which, till now, has been ineffective in treating my cough.

I admit that if it weren't for Dr. Klopstock from Budapest—"the madman," as you refer to him—who I met that frigid February in 1921, I wouldn't even be writing to you now. He takes good care of me, though at times I suspect he's at bottom a hypocrite. He has promised to inject me with sedatives when the pain becomes unbearable; we'll see what happens. Yes, I know there's a vial of camphor ready for me in the medicine chest. Dora Diamant, my dear Dora, trusts him implicitly and that pleases me. They take turns sitting at my side when I can't stay alone. I'm extremely grateful, though I tell them there's no reason to prolong the agony. Guess what? Yesterday late at night an owl perched right outside my window. The bird of death!

You've seen me: 103 pounds fully dressed. I've lost my voice and can only be heard if I whisper—which isn't so bad coming from me. They've suggested that Dora end my treatment and take me home, but she refuses. I'm completely in favor! Dying in a hospital is too impersonal. Furthermore, all this is very expensive—as if one has to pay taxes to a sultan before checking out. Soon I'll get some money from Otto Pick and Prager Presse[1] for the "Josephine" story; also, Die Schmiede owes me a check. If they're sent to you, pass them on to Dora to pay the bills.

When you visited me, we could barely communicate. You claim I was too absorbed, as if hiding a secret, and that my gestures were strange. We talked about my October 22, 1922 request, in which I expressed my final wishes regarding my writings. Since you could make yourself understood and I couldn't I would like to clarify again what I meant: I'll also mention an astonishing and sad development which, I'm afraid, will perhaps disturb our friendship. On the same day of your visit I got the unpleasant news that Dora's father, after consulting with a rabbi, had rejected our wish to marry. But that's another story.

Of all my writings, you know that the only ones of value are *The Trial*, "The Stoker," "The Metamorphosis," "In the Penal Colony," "A Country Doctor," and "A Hunger Artist." (You can save the few remaining copies of *Meditations* since I don't want to give anyone the work of eliminating them—still, none of its stories can be reprinted.) When I say these writings have value, I don't mean to imply they should be reprinted or saved for posterity; on the contrary, my deepest wish would be for them to disappear completely from sight. But everything else in newspapers, magazines, papers, manuscripts, letters—barring nothing—should be retrieved from the people who have them and burned, preferably without being read. I can't stop you from reading them, but I wouldn't like it; in no way should anyone other than you set eyes upon them.

---

[1] Otto Pick and Prager Presse—Kafka's publishers.

You asked me: why destroy writings that are already part of humanity? I apologize for not having known how to answer. At first I thought of telling you it was an impulse, an inexplicable **premonition**.[2] But I understand what you are saying: what is art if not an attempt to transcend death? Isn't art the trace which remains when we are no longer on this earth? That's why I thought of saying that nothing imperfect should survive and what I've written is imperfect, even though I have spent many nights wide awake changing a defective phrase here or there or looking for the right touch of humor. That which is imperfect causes in me great embarrassment. Many times we've discussed Flaubert[3] and his "irritating"—this is your word, dear friend—meticulousness. Doesn't he state in his letters to Turgenev and to his dearly beloved Louise Colet that he spent months, even years, looking for the ideal word, revising a single page over and over? And what is the right word? No one knows. Or better: only God knows.

Now more than ever I understand my hesitancy regarding my Jewish heritage. I yearn for the immemorial time when a library consisted of just the Whole Book,[4] the one that transcribes Suffering, Truth, and the Law. My father Herrmann is true to his religion though he partakes of its rituals mechanically and without question. His severe, authoritarian manner instills terror. It's difficult for me to get close to him and I suppose K.'s[5] indecision and incapacity in *The Castle* is inspired by him. My idea of God is of a distant warden in a state of alertness, always ready to punish. Is this the same God who wrote the Book of Books? If so, he must've written it in a burst of rage, taking pleasure in the dreadfulness of his creations.

---

[2] **premonition**—omen; forewarning.

[3] Flaubert—Gustave Flaubert, a famous 19th-century French writer.

[4] Whole Book—Torah.

[5] K.'s—belonging to a character in *The Castle*.

Now I feel I've mocked my father. Fresh in my mind is the letter I wrote him when you and I were in Schelesin. Remember? I had to tell him about my endless yearning for childhood and the suffering I endured under his implacable yoke. I'm sure the death of the two babies my mother bore after I was born was traumatic; truth is they, not I, deserved to live. I have a clear memory in mind: I was a young boy and, on a night like so many others, I was whining, begging for water. It wasn't only that I was thirsty, I also wanted to enjoy myself. Suddenly my father came in, dragged me out of bed and took me to the balcony. He left me there locked up till I grew calm. That was his style—intolerant and demanding. The event left me scarred. From that day on, I dream about a huge man, a judge who comes to pull me out of my bedroom and condemns me. What I leave behind in my writings is a variation on that dream—a handful of complaints which lack the least bit of interest—the view of a conflicted person. Is there any hope in a kingdom where cats chase after a mouse? Yes, but not for the mouse.

For many years this has been my view: nevertheless, today I feel its hypocrisy and inconsistency. My father always wanted to see me as a successful son, which makes me wonder: Does God perceive us as we are? I'm sure he does. Any other way, then, would be our fault. The weakened and tense relationship with my father is more my fault than his. I take pleasure in playing the role of Jesus Christ—the martyr who suffers for others. Deep down I am an actor specializing in submissive characters. An actor who knows how to create something out of his own being. Is my father truly so severe and authoritarian? Perhaps. Valli, Ottla, and Elli[6] (the latter

---

[6] Valli, Ottla, and Elli—Kafka's sisters.

to a lesser extent) also complain about his character, though they have the benefit of being females. To a larger degree, my father is just like my uncles Philip, Heinrich, and Ludwig, at times even more sensitive than they. Tell me then why aren't any of my cousins—Otto, Oskar, Victor, and the others—afraid? Because I am an impostor who has invented a dark reality. Because I've made a career out of being a victim.

How embarrassing for me to reveal to you at age forty-one my hateful comedy. Did you suspect it already? Of course. Why haven't I burned my own writings? The answer is not cowardice but rather because I'm a person weakened by vanity. Deep inside I know very well you too won't set them ablaze; on the contrary, they're useful to you since your own novels fill you with uncertainty. To achieve a kind of immortality, my books would depend on my own **immolation,**[7] on creating a legend; one would have to read them in the light of all the errors of a poor crucified Jew who detested himself so much. Is there a more fascinating creature than the one who first describes a detestable world and then censures himself?

Now I'm getting to the heart of this letter. Years ago, during the time when I forced myself to learn Hebrew, I met in Studl's boarding house Julie Wohryzek, a beautiful, if a bit foolish, girl. You know the story very well—I've recounted it to you many times, but not its outcome. Her father was a cobbler who also carried out a few administrative tasks in the synagogue. She was neither Jew nor gentile,[8] German nor otherwise. She had a light-hearted spirit; every time we were together, she was laughing. She had been engaged, but her fiancé died in the war. Julie reminded me of Grete Bloch, the woman with whom I had an unhappy romance unbeknownst to my fiancée Felice. I felt both desire and anxiety with Julie.

---

[7] **immolation**—sacrifice by burning, that is, death.

[8] gentile—non-Jew.

Winter brought us together in an old-fashioned room that smelled of ammonia. We were there for a month and a half. Our intimacy, with its implied sexuality, frightened me. Julie did not want to get married and from the start she denied any interest in **procreation.**[9] We were both happy with the relationship; nevertheless, I saw her change in this respect, till she began to yearn for children: she said that being pregnant is "a privilege no woman should renounce." Our first separation was in March of 1919. We reunited in April in Prague and our intimacy grew even more intense. We became engaged and rented an apartment in Wrschowitz. My parents, of course, were against this. Around this time we received copies of "The Penal Colony" from Kurt Wolff Verlag. I remember how with enthusiasm I gave my father one copy. As soon as he saw it, he snuffed my happiness and said with scorn "Put it on my desk!" I felt humiliated. A little later, when I announced in the living room our betrothal, they created a scene. My father **insinuated**[10] that Julie was a common Prague girl—you could tell by her dress and her manners—and my mother agreed without saying a word. All this filled me with doubt, and days later we lost our lease. I decided then to break this—my third— engagement. We separated; Julie, who was twenty-eight years old, was deeply hurt and moved to another city. We separated for a second time, promising to continue writing to each other but didn't. I never heard from her again.

Till a few weeks ago, when I received an airmail letter mailed to my parents' home with no return address. She gave me the astonishing news that my son Zdenek Saul Kafka Wohryzek was four years old. She told me he's a chubby boy with brown eyes and he lost his first tooth in November. He has a scar on his chin

---

[9] **procreation**—having children.
[10] **insinuated**—cleverly suggested.

from when he tripped in school, hitting his head against a sharp metal edge. His mother added that in a few weeks the two of them would be heading off to America. She didn't say a thing about a **reconciliation**.[11]

Did this unsettle me? I gasped for breath and lost my balance. When no one was looking, I burnt the letter. Yes, burned it up. What else could I do? You know very well I could never be a father; to have children is to begin a journey toward redemption, and salvation is not for me but for my **nullity**.[12] Since then I've tried unsuccessfully to put the incident behind me. Furthermore, I'm possessed by an old saying which I repeat day and night till I am worn out. Do you remember it? It's the one about all the crows boasting that just a single crow could destroy the heavens, which proves nothing since the heavens are nothing more than the **negation**[13] of crows. I mentioned this to a German doctor who periodically reexamines me and he smiled, realizing that Kavka means "crow" in Czech.

Wait, there's more. There's a prostitute here among the sanatorium patients and I sit with her on the *terraza*[14] to take some sun. She's a fortuneteller, and one day she wanted to read my future. She took hold of my right hand and opened it. When she saw the lines on my palm, she became suddenly silent, unable to hold back a cry of sorrow. She then assured me that though my own future was dark, my son was in good hands. My heart began to race. I told her I had no offspring but she explained that my son was in excellent health and soon would be arriving in New York. She added that the immigration authorities wouldn't let him enter and he would sail throughout the Caribbean until he reached a port where they spoke Spanish named Veri Crucci or

---

[11] **reconciliation**—making up.

[12] **nullity**—nothingness; nonexistence.

[13] **negation**—in this context, absence or lack.

[14] *terraza*—terrace; patio.

Bara Crutz. And what did his future hold? He would be a merchant. He would begin selling knives and would end up with a successful paint business with a number of stores. A businessman, like his grandfather Herrmann. The former prostitute also said that during his adolescence he would search for me. He would visit my grave in Prague and would reclaim from you, Max, the rights to my books, but that you would ignore him.

Do you know how I felt? Covered with muck, full of filth. (Exactly what I felt when I finished *The Trial*). Dora, to whom I'll never be married, spent the next night at my side. She'll tell you I slept poorly and it's true, I had an awful nightmare. I dreamt that someone was washing my corpse with a soft and oily soap; he wrapped it in a white shroud and chopped it in a thousand pieces with a butcher knife. After he placed the pieces in a hole, I saw you, my parents and brothers, and a policeman writing the following words in stone: Evil does not exist, you have crossed the threshold, everything is fine.

I have the feeling my whole life has been a lie. As if I tried for years to go through a door and not succeeded because the lock seemed **impenetrable**[15] though it really wasn't.

I have a pain in my . . . Will we see each other again? If Zdenek seeks you out, please open the door. Please tell him that I was an actor and executioner.

Franz

---

[15] **impenetrable**—unable to be opened.

QUESTIONS TO CONSIDER

1. In what respects should writers be able to destroy their work, or is their art "the trace which remains when we are no longer on earth," something that rightfully belongs to others?

2. How do you think the narrator's upbringing contributed to his becoming an artist?

3. What do you think "Kafka" means when he writes, "salvation is not for me but for my nullity"?

4. In what way is an artist "an actor and executioner"?

Looking for Some Dignity

BY CLARICE LISPECTOR

Translated by Leland Guyer

*Regarded as one of the greatest female figures in Brazilian litera-
ture, Clarice Lispector (Brazil, 1925–1977) is also internationally
acclaimed. Born in the Ukraine, she lived in the Brazilian state
of Recife before moving to Rio de Janeiro in 1937. Lispector is
known for writing introspective literature in which she repeatedly
questions human nature and mankind's ability to communicate
through language. Among her famous works are* The Passion
According to G.H., Family Ties, *and the essay "Creating Brasília."
In "Looking for Some Dignity" a woman discovers the emptiness
of her life and then struggles desperately to fill it with meaning.*

Mrs. Jorge B. Xavier simply couldn't say how she'd
gotten in. It hadn't been by one of the main gates. She
seemed to have entered in a vague dreaminess through
some kind of narrow opening past some construction

work debris, as if she had crossed obliquely through some opening made just for her. The fact is that when she looked up she was inside.

And when she looked up she saw that she was inside, very much so. She walked endlessly through the underground passages of the Maracana Stadium which seemed to be narrow caverns leading to rooms which occasionally opened out onto the arena through a single window. The stadium, at that scorchingly deserted hour, shimmered beneath the noonday sun, uncommonly hot for the middle of the winter.

So the woman continued down a somber corridor. This one led her to another even more darker. The ceilings of the passages seemed low.

And that corridor there took her to another which in turn took her to another.

The deserted corridor turned. And there she came to another intersection, which took her to another corridor which took her to another intersection.

So she continued mechanically entering corridors which always led to other corridors. Where could the meeting room for the first class be? She had agreed to meet some people there. The lecture might have begun already. She was going to miss it. She didn't allow herself to miss anything "cultural," since this way she stayed young inside. No one on the outside would have guessed she was almost seventy years old. Everyone thought she was around fifty-seven.

But now, lost in the internal dark windings of Maracana, the woman dragged her feet heavily.

It was then that in one of the corridors she suddenly ran into a man who seemed to have sprung from thin air. She asked him about the lecture, but he knew nothing of it. But he did try to find out from another man who suddenly appeared at the turn of the corridor.

The second man said that near the bleachers, on the right in the middle of the open stadium, he'd seen "a gentleman and two ladies, one dressed in red." Mrs. Xavier doubted that these were the people she was to meet before the lecture and, to tell the truth, she had lost sight of the reason she was taking this endless walk. In any case, she followed the man toward the naked, **disgorged**[1] stadium where she stood bleary-eyed in the empty space, in a vast light and a boundless silence, no soccer game, not even a ball. Above all, no crowd. A crowd that made its presence felt through its complete absence.

Had the two ladies and the gentleman already disappeared down some corridor?

The man then said with exaggerated resolve, "I'm going to help you look, and some way or another I'll find those people. They couldn't have just vanished into thin air."

In fact they saw them from way off. But a second later they disappeared again. It seemed to be a child's game whose laughter bit into Mrs. Jorge B. Xavier.

Then she and the man passed through some more corridors. But then this man also disappeared at an intersection.

The woman gave up on the lecture which after all was not very important; not very important, that is, as long as she could finally get out of that scramble of endless paths. Could there not be some exit? She felt as if she were in an elevator stuck between floors. Could there not be some exit?

But all of a sudden she remembered the directions her friend gave on the telephone: "it's fairly near the Maracana Stadium." Remembering this, she understood the hare-brained, distracted way she only half listened, with her other half immersed somewhere else. Mrs. Xavier was very inattentive. So, the meeting was not

---

[1] **disgorged**—empty.

inside Maracanã but near it. Meanwhile her little destiny had willed her to be lost within the **labyrinth.**[2]

Yes, and the battle resumed, even worse now. She really wanted to get out and had no idea which way to go. And once again that man who was looking for the people appeared in the corridor, and once again he guaranteed that he would find them because they could not have disappeared. He said precisely that: "People just don't vanish into thin air."

And the woman said, "You don't need to bother looking any more, all right? It's all right. Thank you very much. The place I'm supposed to meet the people isn't in Maracanã."

The man stopped immediately to look at her, with wonder. "So what are you doing here?"

She wanted to explain that her life was just like that, but she did not know what she meant by "like that" or "her life," and she said nothing. The man repeated the question, feeling curious and at the same time wishing to be discreet: what was she doing there? Nothing, she answered to herself, about to drop from fatigue. But she did not answer him. Instead she let him think she was crazy. Besides, she never explained herself to anyone. She knew that the man thought she was crazy—and who wouldn't? Wasn't she shamefully feeling what she just referred to as "that"? She felt this even though she knew how to keep her mental health on a **par**[3] with her physical health. Her physical health now exhausted, she shuffled through the labyrinth on high-mileage feet. Her way of the cross. She was sweating and suffocating, dressed in very heavy wool during the unseasonably severe summer heat, that summer day misfiled in the winter. Her legs hurt; they hurt under the weight of the

---

[2] **labyrinth**—maze.

[3] **par**—equal level.

old cross. By now she had, in a sense, resigned herself to never leaving Maracana and dying there from her weak heart.

Then, as always, it was only after giving up our dreams that they come true. Suddenly an idea occurred to her: "What an old dummy I am!" Why, instead of looking for people who aren't here, didn't she find that man and find out how to get out of those corridors? All she really wanted was to get out and not run into anyone.

Finally, she found the man coming around a corner. And she spoke to him in a voice turned somewhat tremulous and hoarse from fatigue and the fear that everything was in vain. The discreet man agreed immediately that it was certainly better that she go home and told her carefully, "You seem to be a little confused. Perhaps it's this terrible heat."

Saying this, the man then simply turned with her into the first corridor and at the corner they saw the two large open gates. Just like that? Was it so easy?

Just like that.

Then it occurred to her that she was the only one who could not find the exit, although she did not go on to draw any further conclusions. Mrs. Xavier was just a little frightened and at the same time accustomed to this. There's no doubt that each one of us has an endless road to travel, making this a part of our destiny, something she wasn't sure she believed in.

A taxi was passing by. She hailed it and told the driver with a controlled voice that she was getting older and more tired.

"Driver, I'm not sure of the address. I've forgotten it. But what I do know is that the house is on some street or another that has something to do with Gusmao, and it intersects a street which if I'm not mistaken is called Colonel-what's-his-name."

The driver was as patient as if he were with a child. "Well, don't you worry about a thing. We're calmly going to find a street that has Gusmao in the middle and Colonel at its end," he said turning around with a smile and a conniving wink of his eye that seemed indecent. They drove off with such a bouncing that her belly shook.

Suddenly she spotted and joined the people she was looking for on a sidewalk in front of a large house. It was, however, as if the aim were just to get there and not to listen to a talk which she had forgotten altogether by that time. Mrs. Xavier had lost sight of her objective. And she did not know why she had walked so far. She saw that she had worn herself out beyond her limits, and she wanted to get out of there. The lecture was a nightmare. She then asked an important and vaguely known woman who had a car with a driver to take her home, because she was not feeling good with all this unusual heat. The driver would be there an hour from then. Mrs. Xavier then sat down in a chair they had placed for her in the corridor. She sat there stiffly in her tight girdle, removed from the culture which was unfolding in the closed hall, from which there came not a sound. Now "culture" meant little to her. And there she was in the labyrinths for sixty seconds and for sixty minutes which would lead her to an hour.

The important woman arrived and told her her ride was waiting outside, but that since she was feeling so bad and the chauffeur would take a long time, she had stopped the first taxi that passed by. Why hadn't Mrs. Xavier herself had the idea of calling a taxi, instead of submitting to the **vagaries**[4] of waiting? Mrs. Jorge B. Xavier thanked her with exaggerated courtesy. The woman was always very courteous and well-behaved. She got into the taxi and said, "Leblon, if you please."

---

[4] **vagaries**—unpredictabilities.

Her mind was blank. It seemed her brain was fasting.

After a while she noted that they drove and drove but once again they kept returning to the same plaza. Why didn't they get anywhere? Once again, was there no way out? The driver finally confessed that he didn't know the south side of Rio and that he only worked in the north. And she didn't know how to tell him the way. The cross she bore for years weighed more and more, and absence of an exit simply revived the black magic of the Maracana corridors. There was no way to get free from the plaza! Then the driver told her to take another taxi, and he even beckoned one over to their side. She thanked him coolly; she observed the social graces, even with those she knew well. More than this, she was very kind. In the next cab she said fearfully, "If it's all right with you, could we go to Leblon?"

And they simply left the plaza and drove through other streets.

It was on opening the door to her apartment with her key that she imagined that she wanted to cry out loud. But she wasn't one to sob or complain. She informed the maid in passing that she wouldn't take any telephone calls. She went straight to her bedroom, removed all her clothes, took a pill with no water and waited for it to take effect.

In the meantime she smoked. She remembered that it was the month of August, and they say that August is bad luck. But September would come one day, like a way out. And September was in some ways like the month of May: a lighter and more transparent month. She was vaguely thinking about this when drowsiness finally came, and she fell asleep.

Hours later, when she woke up she saw that a fine, cold rain was falling; the cold was like the edge of a knife. Naked in bed, she was freezing. And she thought how an old naked lady was quite odd. She recalled that she had planned to buy a woolen shawl. She glanced at the clock: she'd still find businesses open. She got a cab and said, "Ipanema, if you please."

"What's that? The Botanical Garden?" the man asked.

"Ipanema, please," the woman repeated, quite surprised. It was the absurdity of the complete lack of communication: after all, what did the words "Ipanema" and "Botanical Garden" have in common? But again she vaguely thought that "that's just how her life was."

She made another purchase quickly and saw herself in the street, now dark, with nothing to do, since Mr. Jorge B. Xavier had traveled to São Paulo the day before and wouldn't return until the day after.

Then, again at home, between taking another sleeping pill or doing something else, she opted for the second, remembering that she could return to look for the lost bill of exchange. What little she understood of it was that that piece of paper represented money. Two days ago she searched the whole house carefully, including the kitchen, but in vain. Now it occurred to her, why not under the bed? Perhaps. She kneeled on the floor. But being on her knees quickly tired her out, and she bent down and leaned on her two hands.

She then noticed that she was on all fours.

And so she stayed for a while, perhaps meditating, perhaps not. Who knows, Mrs. Xavier might have tired of being human. She was a dog on four feet. With no dignity whatsoever. Her pride a thing of the past. On all fours, a little pensive perhaps. But under the bed there was just dust.

She stood up with some effort, caused by her stiff joints, and saw that there was nothing more to do but consider realistically—and it was only with painful effort that she could view reality—that the letter was lost and that to continue looking for it would be the same as never getting out of Maracana.

And just as always, as soon as she stopped looking, as she opened her hanky drawer to pull one out—there was the letter of exchange.

Then the woman, tired from the effort of being on all fours, sat on the bed and for no apparent reason began to cry softly. It seemed more like a monotonous Arabian chant. She hadn't cried for over thirty years, but she was so tired now. If this was indeed crying. It wasn't. It was something. Finally she blew her nose. Then she thought that she would take her fate in hand and improve it somehow. "Where there's a will there's a way," she mused (without actually believing it). And all this about being a slave to a destiny occurred to her because without wanting to, she'd already begun thinking about "that."

But it happens that the woman also thought: it was too late to have a destiny. She thought that any kind of switch with another human being would do her good. It was then that it occurred to her that there was no one else with whom she could trade places. Despite what she would wish, she was who she was and couldn't become another. Each one was unique. Mrs. Jorge B. Xavier was unique too.

But everything that occurred to her was preferable to being "that." And that came from her long exitless corridors. "That," now with no sense of decency, was the painful hunger of her insides, the hunger of being possessed by the **unattainable**[5] television idol. She never missed his television program. Now that she couldn't stop thinking about him, the trick was to allow herself to think about and recall the girlish face of Roberto Carlos, my love.

---

[5] **unattainable**—unobtainable.

She went to wash her dusty hands and saw herself in the wash basin mirror. Then Mrs. Xavier thought, "If I want him a lot, really a lot, he'll be mine for at least one night." She believed vaguely in the force of the will. She got tangled up again in choked and twisted desire.

But, who knows? If she gave up on Roberto Carlos, then things between him and her would happen. Mrs. Xavier meditated a bit on the matter. Then she cleverly pretended to give up on Roberto Carlos. But she knew well that the magical abandonment only gave positive results when it was true, and not just a trick as a means to an end. Reality required a lot of the woman. She examined herself in the mirror to see if her face would turn hideous under the sway of her feelings. But it was a quiet face which long ago had ceased revealing her feelings. Besides, her face never expressed anything but good upbringing. And now it was just the mask of a seventy year old woman. Then her lightly made–up face seemed clown-like to her. The woman made a half-hearted attempt to smile to see if it would help. It didn't.

On the outside—she saw it in the mirror—she was dry, like a dried fig. But inside she wasn't parched. On the contrary. Inside she was like moist gums, soft like toothless gums.

She then pursued a thought that might spiritualize her or dry her up once and for all. But she'd never been spiritual. And because of Roberto Carlos the woman was wrapped up in the darkness of the matter where she was profoundly anonymous.

Standing in the bathroom she was as anonymous as a chicken.

In a split second she unconsciously glimpsed that everyone was anonymous. Because no one is the other and the other didn't know the other. Then that person is anonymous. And now she was tangled in that deep and mortal well, in the body's rebellion. Body of invisible depths in which the rats and lizards of her instincts scurried about veiled in malignant shadows. And was everything out of time, fruit out of season? Why hadn't the other old women advised her that this could happen until the end? In old men she had seen many **lecherous**[6] eyes. But not in old women. Out of season. And she was alive, as if she were someone, she who was no one.

Mrs. Jorge B. Xavier was no one.

And she wanted to have beautiful romantic feelings about the delicacy of Roberto Carlos's face, but she couldn't. His delicacy just took her to a dark corridor of sensuality. And the damage was **lasciviousness.**[7] It was a vulgar hunger. She wanted to consume the mouth of Roberto Carlos. She wasn't romantic, she was ill-informed on the subject of love. There, in the bathroom, before the wash basin mirror.

With the indelible mark of age.

Without even one sublime thought to serve as a **rudder**[8] and ennoble her existence.

Then she began to undo her French knot and to comb her hair slowly. She had to dye it soon; her white roots were showing now. Then the woman thought: never in my life have I had a climax as in the stories you read. The climax was Roberto Carlos.

She thought. She concluded that she was going to die as secretly as she had lived. But she also knew that every death is secret.

From the bottom of her future death she imagined she saw the **coveted**[9] image of Roberto Carlos in the mirror, with that soft curly hair of his. There she was, a

---

[6] **lecherous**—lustful.

[7] **lasciviousness**—desire.

[8] **rudder**—guiding force.

[9] **coveted**—desired; envied.

prisoner of desire as out of season as a summer day in midwinter. A prisoner in the tangle of corridors of Maracana. A prisoner of the mortal secret of old women. It's just that she wasn't used to being almost seventy years old. She lacked practice and didn't have the least bit of experience.

"My dear little Roberto Carlos," she said loudly and quite alone.

And she added: my love. Her voice sounded strange to her as if with no sense of decency or shame it were the first time she were confessing that which after all should have been shameful. The woman imagined that it was possible that little Roberto might not wish to accept her love because she herself was aware that this love was silly, **saccharinely**[10] **voluptuous,**[11] and **gluttonous.**[12] And Roberto Carlos seemed so pure, so sexless.

Would her lightly colored lips still be kissable? Or would it, perhaps, be repugnant to kiss the mouth of an old woman? Showing no emotion, she examined her lips carefully. And still showing no emotion, she softly sang the refrain from Roberto Carlos's most famous song: "Warm me this winter night, and everything else can go to hell."

It was then that Mrs. Jorge B. Xavier abruptly doubled over the sink as though she were going to vomit out her **viscera**[13] and she interrupted her life with an explosive silence: there!—has!—to!—be!—a—way—out!

---

[10] **saccharinely**—too sweetly.

[11] **voluptuous**—sensual; physical.

[12] **gluttonous**—greedy.

[13] **viscera**—bowels; internal organs.

QUESTIONS TO CONSIDER

1. What do you think would explain Mrs. Xavier's confusion?

2. In what kind of cultural pursuits do you think Mrs. Xavier engages, and how important do you think they have been to her?

3. What do you think of Mrs. Xavier's assessment of her predicament as being "just how life is"?

4. What is it that Mrs. Xavier would like to escape at the end of the story? What way out might she find?

Park Cinema

BY ELENA PONIATOWSKA

Translated by Teres Mendeth-Faith and Elisabeth Heinicke

Elena Poniatowska (Mexico, 1933–) is a prolific journalist, novelist, and biographer. She is the author of such famous works as Tinísima, a fictionalized biography of Italian photographer Tina Modotti, and of Massacre in Mexico, a testimonial narrative about the 1968 student uprising in Mexico City. Much of Poniatowska's work deals with social issues and the influence of popular culture in particular. In "Park Cinema," a crazed fan writes to his favorite film actress, whose stardom has blinded his view of reality.

Señorita:

As of today, you will have to strike my name from the list of your admirers. Perhaps I ought not to inform you of this decision, but to do so would be to betray a personal integrity that has never shied away from the **exigencies**[1] of the Truth. By thus divorcing myself from

---

[1] **exigencies**—urgent requirements.

you, I am acting in accordance with a profound change in spirit, which leads me to the decision never again to number myself among the viewers of your films.

This afternoon—or rather, this evening—you have destroyed me. I do not know whether this matters to you, but I am a man shattered to pieces. Do you understand what I am saying? A devotee who has followed your image on the screens of first-run houses and neighborhood theaters, a loving critic who would justify the very worst of your moral behavior, I now swear on my knees to renounce you forever, though a mere poster from *Forbidden Fruit* is enough to shake my resolve. As you may see, I am yet a man seduced by appearances.

Comfortably **ensconced**[2] in my seat I was one in a multitude, a creature lost in an anonymous darkness, who suddenly felt himself caught up in a personal sadness, bitter and inescapable. It was then that I was truly myself, the loner who suffers and now addresses you. For no brotherly hand reached to touch mine. While you were calmly destroying my heart on the screen, all those around me stayed passionately true. Yes, there was even one scoundrel who laughed shamelessly while I watched you swoon in the arms of that abominable suitor who dragged you to the final extremes of human degradation.

And let me ask you this, señorita: Is he worthless whose every ideal is suddenly lost?

You will say I am a dreamer, an eccentric, one of those meteorites that fall to earth against all calculated odds. You may dispense with your hypotheses: it is I who is judging you, and do me the favor of taking greater responsibility for your actions, and before you sign a contract or accept a co-star, do consider that a man such as I might be among your future audience and

---

[2] **ensconced**—settled; lodged.

might receive a fatal blow. It is not jealousy that makes me speak this way, but, believe me: in *Slaves of Desire*, you were kissed, caressed and assaulted to excess.

I do not know whether my memory makes me exaggerate, but in the cabaret[3] scene there was no reason for you to half-open your lips in that way, to let your hair down over your shoulders, and to tolerate the impudent manners of that sailor who yawns as he leaves you, who abandons you like a sinking ship after he has drowned your honor on the bed.

I know that actors owe a debt to their audience; that they, in a sense, relinquish their free will and give themselves up to the capricious desires of a perverse director; moreover, I know that they are obliged to follow point by point all the deficiencies and inconsistencies of the script they must bring to life, but let me state that everyone, even in the worst of **contingencies**,[4] retains a minimum of initiative, a fragment of freedom—and you could not or chose not to exercise it.

If you were to take the trouble, you might say in your defense that the very things I am accusing you of today you have done ever since your screen debut. True, and I am ashamed to admit that I cannot justify my feelings. I undertook to love you just as you are. Pardon—as I imagined you to be. Like anyone who has ever been disillusioned, I curse the day that linked my life with your **cinematographic**[5] destiny. And I want to make clear that I accepted you when you were an obscure newcomer, when no one had ever heard of you, when they gave you the part of that streetwalker with crooked stockings and worn-down heels, a part no decent woman could have accepted. Nonetheless I forgave you, and in that dirty and indifferent theater I hailed the birth of a star. It was I who discovered you,

---

[3] cabaret—nightclub; bistro.

[4] **contingencies**—circumstances.

[5] **cinematographic**—relating to the movies.

I was the only one who could perceive your soul, immaculate as it was despite your torn handbag and your sheepish manner. By what is dearest to you in the world? Forgive the bluntness of my outburst.

Your mask has slipped, señorita. I have come to see the **vileness**[6] of your deceit. You are not that creature of delights, that tender, fragile dove I had grown used to, that swallow innocent in flight, your face in my dreams hidden by a lacy veil—no, you are a tramp through and through, the dregs of the earth, a passing fancy in the worst sense of the word. From this moment on, my dear señorita, you must go your way and I mine. Go on, go, keep walking the streets, I have already drowned in your sewer like a rat. But I must stress that I continue to address you as "señorita" solely because, in spite of the blows you have dealt me, I am still a gentleman. My saintly old mother had instilled in my innermost being the importance of always keeping up appearances. Images linger, my life as well. Hence . . . señorita. Take it, if you will, as a sort of desperate irony.

I have seen you lavish kisses and receive caresses in hundreds of films, but never before did you receive your fortunate partner into your spirit. You kissed with simplicity like any good actress: as one would kiss a cardboard cutout. For—and I wish to make this clear once and for all—the only worthwhile sensuality is that which involves the soul, for the soul surrounds our body as the skin of the grape its pulp, as the peel contains the juice within. Before now, your love scenes did not upset me, for you always preserved a shred of dignity albeit profaned;[7] I was always aware of an intimate rejection, a last-minute withdrawal that redeemed my anguish and consoled my lament. But in *Rapture in the Body*, your eyes moist with love, you showed me your

---

[6] **vileness**—badness; foulness.

[7] **albeit profaned**—even though defiled and unclean.

true face, the one I never wish to see again. Go on, confess it: you really are in love with the scoundrel, that second-rate flash-in-the-pan comedian, aren't you? What avails an impudent denial? At least every word of mine, every promise I made, was true: and every one of your movements was the expression of a spirit that had surrendered itself. Why did you toy with me the way they all do? Why did you deceive me like all women deceive, wearing one different mask after another? Why would you not reveal all at once, in the beginning, the detestable face that now torments me?

This drama of mine is practically **metaphysical**,[8] and I can find no possible solution. I am alone in the nighttime of my delirium. Well, all right, my wife does understand me completely, and at times she even shares in my distress. We were still revelling in the sweet delights appropriate to newlyweds when, our defenses down, we saw the first of your films. Do you still remember it? The one about the dumb athletic diver who ended up at the bottom of the sea because of you, wetsuit and all. I left the theater completely deranged and it would have been futile effort to try to keep it from my wife. But at least she was completely on my side, and had to admit that your **deshabilles**[9] were truly splendid. Nor did she find it inconvenient to accompany me to the cinema six more times, believing in good faith that the enchantment would be broken by routine. But, alas, things grew worse with every new film of yours that opened. Our family budget underwent serious modifications in order to permit cinema attendance on the order of three times a week. And it goes without saying that after each cinematographic session we spent the rest of the night arguing. All the same, my mate did not get ruffled. For after all, you were but a defenseless

---

[8] **metaphysical**—mystical; spiritual.
[9] **deshabilles**—intentionally careless ways.

shadow, a two-dimensional **silhouette,**[10] subject to the deficiencies of light. And my wife good-naturedly accepted as her rival a phantom whose appearance could be controlled at will, although she wasted no opportunity to have a good laugh at our expense. I remember her pleasure on the fatal night when, due to technical difficulties, you spoke for a good ten minutes with an inhuman voice, almost that of a robot, going from a **falsetto**[11] to deepest bass. And while we're on the subject of your voice, I would have you know that I set myself to studying French because I could not resign myself to the abridged subtitles in Spanish, colorless and misleading. I learned to decipher the melodious sound of your voice, and with that accomplishment came the intolerable scourge of hearing atrocious words directed at your person or issuing from your very lips. I longed for the time when these words had reached me by way of a **priggish**[12] translation; now, they were slaps in the face.

The most serious aspect to this whole thing is that my wife is showing disquieting signs of ill-humor. Allusions to you and to your on-screen conduct are more and more frequent and ferocious. Lately she has concentrated on your intimate apparel and tells me that I am talking in vain to a woman of no substance. And sincerely now, just between ourselves, why this profusion of infamous transparency, this wasteful display of intimate bits of filmy acetate? When the only thing I want to find in you is that little sparkle, sad and bitter, that you once had in your eyes . . . But let's get back to my wife. She makes faces and mimics you. She makes fun of me too. Mockingly, she echoes some of my most heart-rending sighs. "Those kisses that pained me in *Unforgettable You* still burn me like fire." Wherever we

---

[10] **silhouette**—outline; shadow.

[11] **falsetto**—high pitch.

[12] **priggish**—prissy; proper.

may be, she is wont to speak of you; she says we must confront this problem from a purely rational angle, from a scientific point of view, and she comes up with absurd but potent arguments. She does no less than claim you are not real and that she herself is an actual woman. And by dint of[13] proving it to me, she is demolishing my illusions one by one. I do not know what will happen to me if what is so far only a rumor should turn out to be the truth: that you will come here to make a film, that you will honor our country with a visit. For the love of God, by the holiest of holies—stay where you are, señorita!

No, I do not want to go see you again, for every time the music dies away and the action fades from the screen, I am overwhelmed. I'm speaking of that fatal barrier represented by the three cruel letters that put an end to the modest measure of happiness of my nights of love, at two pesos apiece. Bit by bit I have relinquished the desire to stay and live with you on film, and I no longer die of pain as I am towed away from the cinema by my wife, who has the bad habit of getting up as soon as the last frame has passed. Señorita, I leave you here. I do not even ask you for an autograph, for should you ever send me one I would be capable of forgetting your unpardonable treason. Please accept this letter as the final act of homage of a devastated soul, and forgive me for including you in my dreams. Yes, more than one night I dreamt about you, and there is nothing that I have to envy those fly-by-night lovers who collect a salary to hold you in their arms and ply you with borrowed eloquence.

Your humble servant
P.S.

---

[13] by dint of—by force of.

I had neglected to tell you that I am writing from behind bars. This letter would never have reached your hands, had I not feared that the world would give you an erroneous account of me. For the newspapers (which always twist things around) are taking advantage of this ridiculous event: "Last night, an unknown man, either drunk or mentally deranged, interrupted a showing of *Slaves of Desire* at its most stirring point, when he ripped the screen of the Park Cinema by plunging a knife in the breast of Françoise Arnoul. In spite of the darkness, three members of the audience saw the maniac rush towards the actress brandishing a knife, and they got out of their seats to get a better look at him so they could identify him at the time of arraignment. This was easily done, as the individual collapsed once the crime had been committed."

I know that it's impossible, but I would give anything for you to remember always that sharp stab in your breast.

QUESTIONS TO CONSIDER

1. For what offense does the narrator take the actress to task? What do you think she has really done?

2. Why do you think the narrator says the only thing he hopes to find in the image of his beloved is a sad, bitter sparkle she once had in her eyes? What does this mean to him?

3. What message does Poniatowska convey about the role of cinema and its ability to distort people's understanding of reality?

ACKNOWLEDGEMENTS

8 From "Roundels" by Sor Juana Inés de La Cruz, from *Poems, Protest, and a Dream: Selected Writings by Sor Juana Inés de La Cruz,* translated by Margaret Sayers Peden.

12 Reprinted with the permission of Scribner, a Division of Simon & Schuster Inc. from *The Stories of Eva Luna* by Isabel Allende, translated from the Spanish by Margaret Sayers Peden. Copyright © 1989 Isabel Allende. English translation copyright © 1991 Macmillan Publishing Company.

24 "The Warmth of Things" by Nélida Piñón, translated by Helen Lane, published in Portugese as "O calor das coisas" in O calor das coisas: contos (Editora Nova Froneira, 1980). Copyright © 1980 by Nélida Piñón. Reprinted by permission of Agencia Literaria Carmen Balcells S.A.

32 Calvert Casey, "A Little Romance," in *Calvert Casey: The Collected Stories,* trans. John H. R. Polt, ed. Ilan Stavans. Copyright 1998, Duke University Press. All rights reserved. Reprinted with permission.

46 "The Tree" by María Luisa Bombal translated by Richard Cunningham and Lucia Guerra is reprinted with permission from the publisher of *Short Stories by Latin American Women: The Magic and the Real,* compiled and edited by Celia Correas de Zapata (Houston: Arte Público Press–University of Houston, 1990).

66 From *A Sarmiento Anthology,* translated from the Spanish by Stuart Edgar Grummon, edited by Allison Williams Bunkley. Copyright © 1948 and renewed 1976 by Princeton University Press. Reprinted by permission of Princeton University Press.

80 "Mexican Masks" (pp. 29–46) from *The Labyrinth of Solitude* by Octavio Paz, translated from the Spanish by Lysander Kemp, Yara Milos, and Rachel Phillips Belash. Copyright © 1962 by Grove Press, Inc. Used by permission of Grove/Atlantic, Inc.

93 "Ode to the onion" by Pablo Neruda is reprinted by permission from *Neruda's Garden: An Anthology of Odes* translated by María Jacketti, Latin American Literary Review Press, 1995.

97 "The Lamp," "The Brazier," "The Earthen Jar" by Gabriela Mistral. *Some Spanish American Poets,* translated by Alice Stone Blackwell, with an introduction and notes by Isaac Goldberg, Ph.D. New York: D. Appleton and Century, 1929.

102 From "Balthazar's Marvelous Afternoon" from *No One Writes to the Colonel...* by Gabriel García Márquez. Copyright © 1968 in the English translation by HarperCollins Publishers, Inc. Reprinted by permission of HarperCollins Publishers, Inc.

113 "The Return" from *The Selected Poems of Rosario Castellanos,* translated by Magda Bogin, edited by Cecilia Vicuna & Magda Bogin. Reprinted by permission of Magda Bogin.

130 "The Feather Pillow" from *The Decapitated Chicken and Other Stories* by Horacio Quiroga, translated by Margaret Sayers Peden. Copyright

© 1976 by the University of Texas Press. Reprinted by permission of the publisher.

136 "Axolotl" from *End of the Game and Other Stories* by Julio Cortázar, translated by Paul Blackburn. Copyright © 1967 by Random House, Inc. Reprinted by permission of Pantheon Books, a division of Random House, Inc.

144 Reprinted from *The Burning Plain and Other Stories* by Juan Rulfo, translated by George D. Schade. Copyright © 1953, translation Copyright © 1967, renewed 1996. By permission of the University of Texas Press.

155 "The Third Bank of the River" from *The Third Bank of the River* by Joao Guimarães Rosa, trans., Barbara Shelby. Copyright © 1968 by Alfred A. Knopf, Inc. Reprinted by permission of Alfred A. Knopf, a Division of Random House, Inc.

163 "The Eclipse" from *Complete Works and Other Stories* by Augusto Monterroso, translated by Edith Grossman. Copyright © 1995. By permission of the University of Texas Press.

166 "Bottles," from *Intoxicada* by Alcina Lubitch Domecq. Copyright © 1988 by Alcina Lubitch Domecq. English translation 1995 by Ilan Stavans. Reprinted with permission of Ilan Stavans.

174–178 Victor Englebert

180 "The Secret Miracle", from *Collected Fictions* by Jorge Luis Borges, translated by Andrew Hurley, copyright © 1998 by Maria Kodama; translation copyright © 1998 by Penguin Putnam Inc. Used by permission of Viking Penguin, a division of Penguin Putnam Inc.

190 "A Heaven Without Crows" from *The One-Handed Pianist and Other Stories* by Ilan Stavans. Copyright © 1996. Reprinted with permission of the University of New Mexico Press.

200 "Looking for Some Dignity" by Clarice Lispector translated by Leland Guyer is reprinted with permission from the publisher of *Short Stories by Latin American Women: The Magic and the Real*, compiled and edited by Celia Correas de Zapata (Houston: Arte Público Press–University of Houston, 1990).

213 "Park Cinema" by Elena Poniatowska translated by Teres Mendeth-Faith and Elisabeth Heinicke is reprinted with permission from the publisher of *Short Stories by Latin American Women: The Magic and the Real*, compiled and edited by Celia Correas de Zapata (Houston: Arte Público Press–University of Houston, 1990).

Photos 61 *top* Photo Courtesy of María del Perpetuo Socorro Villarreal Escarrega. Coordinación Nacional de Asuntos Jurídicos del INAH; **61–63** AP/Wide World Photos; **116–122, 170–172, 177–178** Victor Englebert; **119, 169, 173, 175** Chip and Rosa María de la Cueva Petersen; **121** *upper right* Bettman/Corbis; **123** *bottom* Corbis/Bettmann; **124–125** Bettmann/Corbis; **126** Afp/Corbis; **127** David Kennerly/Corbis; **128** Enzo & Paolo Ragazzini/Corbis.

Every effort has been made to secure complete rights and permissions for each selection presented herein. Updated acknowledgments, if needed, will appear in subsequent printings.

Index